HBJ BOOKMARK READING PROGRAM

Margaret Early

Elizabeth K. Cooper

Nancy Santeusanio

People and Places

HARCOURT BRACE JOVANOVICH

New York   Chicago   San Francisco   Atlanta   Dallas   and   *London*

Printed in the United States of America   ISBN 0-15-331783-3

ACKNOWLEDGMENTS: For permission to reprint copyrighted material, grateful acknowledgment is made to the following sources:

Linda Allen. Adaptation of "Mrs. Simkin's Bed" by Linda Allen originally appeared in *Cricket* magazine, March, 1976. Copyright © 1976 by Linda Allen.
Atheneum Publishers "Shells" from *I Thought I Heard the City* by Lilian Moore. Text copyright © 1969 by Lilian Moore.
Jim Copp: Lyrics to "Martha Matilda O'Toole" from the Playhouse Records album *Jim Copp Tales,* produced by Jim Copp and Ed Brown.
E. P. Dutton and Curtis Brown Ltd., London, as Agent for the Estate of A. A. Milne "Swing Song" and "Wind on the Hill" from *Now We Are Six* by A. A. Milne. Copyright 1927 by E. P. Dutton; renewal © 1955 by A. A. Milne.
Harper & Row, Publishers, Inc.: Poem 13 from *Any Me I Want to Be: Poems by Karla Kuskin.* Copyright © 1972 by Karla Kuskin. "The Worst" from *Where the Sidewalk Ends* by Shel Silverstein. Copyright © 1974 by Shel Silverstein. "The Wheels of the Bus" from *What Shall We Do and Allee Balloo!* collected and edited by Marie Winn, musical arrangements by Allan Miller. Copyright © 1970 by Marie Winn and Allan Miller.
Phyllis Krasilovsky: Adaptation of *Benny's Flag* by Phyllis Krasilovsky (retitled: "The Big Dipper"). Copyright © 1960 by Phyllis Krasilovsky.
James and Ruth McCrea: Adaptation of "Olaf and the Dragon" from *The Story of Olaf* by James and Ruth McCrea. Copyright © 1964 by James and Ruth McCrea.
Parents' Magazine Press: Adaptation of *The Flying Shoes* by Cynthia Jameson. Text copyright © 1973 by Cynthia Jameson.
G. P. Putnam's Sons and the author: Adaptation of *Herbert's Treasure* by Alice Low. Copyright © 1971 by Alice Low.
Ray Sipherd: Adaptation of *The White Kite* by Ray Sipherd, published by Bradbury Press.
Franklin Watts, Inc.: Adaptation of *Racing on the Wind* by E. and R. S. Radlauer. Copyright © 1974 by E. and R. S. Radlauer.

Don Almquist: 72–80; Yvette Banek: 237–251; Kevin Callahan: 10–19; Cary: 150–154; Eulala Conner: 81–91; Kinuko Craft: 35–38; Jerry Dior: 104–110; Creston Ely: 195–200; Pamela Ford: 194; Arthur Friedman: 28, 34, 155; Jüng Furrer: 61–71; Robert T. Handville: 98–103; Margaret Hathaway: 170–185; Robin Hotchkiss: 61–64, 93–96, 126–128, 188–192, 221–224; Ingrid Koepcke: 236; Robert Lo Grippo: 20–25, 45–50; Ken Longtemps: 148–149; Phyllis Luch: 7, 65, 97, 129, 193, 225; Sal Murdocca: 8–9, 138–147; Diane Patterson: 111–117; Alan Reingold: 130–137; Ruth Sanderson: 118–125; Monica Santa: 51–60, 201–215; Charles Schulz: 168–169; Robert Vann Nutt: 216–220; Sam Q. Weisman: 40–44, 186–187

COVER: John Des Jardins/DPI

HBJ PHOTOS: Page 29; 33; 35; 66; 92; 228; 231; 232; 233; 234; 235

Page 26, Russ Kinne/Photo Researchers; 155, Gene Ahrens/Bruce Coleman; 156, E. M. Bordis/Leo de Wys; 157, E. M. Bordis/Leo de Wys; 158, Frank T. Wood/Focus on Sports; 159, Fred de Wys/Leo de Wys; 160, E. M. Bordis/Leo de Wys; 161, Jim Pond/Shostal; 162–162, W. Ostgathe/Leo de Wys; 164, Harvey Shaman/Globe Photos; 165, E. M. Bordis/Leo de Wys; 166, Jerry Wachter/Focus on Sports; 167, Jim Goodwin/Photo Researchers; 229, Smithsonian Institution; 230 (top), Smithsonian Institution; 230 (bottom), Irwin Weinberg Rareties.

Contents

The World of Giants and Monsters

(To be read by the teacher.)

The Worst

When singing songs of scariness,
Of bloodiness and hairyness,
I feel obligated at this moment to
    remind you
Of the most ferocious beast of all:

8

Three thousand pounds and nine
feet tall—
The Glurpy Slurpy Skakagrall—
Who's standing right behind you.

SHEL SILVERSTEIN

OLAF AND THE DRAGON

by JAMES and RUTH McCREA

Many years ago, two brave knights lived in an old castle. They were named Sir Charles and Sir Egbert. With them lived a boy named Olaf.

Sir Charles and Sir Egbert had fine days riding horses and being brave. Olaf ran after birds and rabbits. Their castle was not big or grand. But they were happy.

10

Deep in the dark woods, not far from the castle, lived a giant dragon. The dragon roared all day and all night. Its great roar made the children cry. It scared the people so, they could not sleep at night.

One morning, after a very bad night, Sir Charles said to them, "This has to stop! Are we not the bravest knights for miles around?"

"We are the only knights for miles around," said Sir Egbert.

"Then it is up to us to get rid of that dragon!" said Sir Charles.

"Oh my!" said Sir Egbert.

"I know how to do it," said Sir Charles. "We must go see the wizard at his store."

Olaf got horses, and off they went.

They soon met the wizard. Sir Charles said, "Turn us into dragons!"

The wizard looked up in surprise.

"Why dragons?" the wizard asked.

"To kill a dragon," said Sir Charles.

"You know that it takes a dragon to kill a dragon," said Sir Egbert.

The wizard looked at them for a long time. "I can turn you into dragons, all right," he said. "But I'm not so sure that's the best way."

But the two knights asked again and again. "All right," said the wizard at last. He took down a small green jar.

"This is magic water," he said.
"Drink a little of it before bed. In the
morning you will be dragons."

The three thanked the wizard. As
they were leaving the store, the wizard
said something softly into Olaf's ear.
He said, "Remember. You must fight as
a person, not as a dragon. Only then
will the magic water do its magic."

Olaf thanked the wizard again.
Holding the magic water with great
care, Olaf went with the knights back
to the castle.

13

That night, after Olaf went to sleep, Sir Charles opened the jar. Each of the knights took some of the magic water.

The two knights left Olaf in the castle. They went off into the dark woods.

All night they waited. In the morning they were dragons! They knew what they had to do.

14

The two knights, who were now dragons, ran to the cave of the roaring dragon. After a long fight, the roaring dragon fell down. It had been killed.

But now two dragons, not one, sat roaring in the woods. And no brave knights were around to fight them!

Olaf got up. He was all by himself. He knew what had happened, but did not know what to do about it.

Then he saw the green jar. Some of the magic water was still in it. All at once, Olaf remembered the wizard's words. "YOU MUST FIGHT AS A PERSON, NOT AS A DRAGON. ONLY THEN WILL THE MAGIC WATER DO ITS MAGIC."

Olaf picked up the green jar and set out for the woods. He tried to be brave.

16

Olaf soon found the two dragons. After the great fight, they were sleeping. Olaf went nearer . . . and nearer . . . and nearer.

When he was next to the dragons, he took out the magic water. He let some of it fall on each dragon.

All at once the dragons opened their eyes. They roared. Fire shot into the air. Olaf did not want to get burned! He ran!

Olaf ran until he could not run any more. He fell down on the grass and soon was sleeping.

After a time, the magic water worked its magic. Sir Charles and Sir Egbert walked out of the woods. They were knights once again.

They found Olaf sleeping in the grass. The knights picked him up. They took Olaf, who was still sleeping, back to the castle.

Sir Charles said, "We were brave to fight the dragon. But Olaf was far braver. He had to fight two dragons as a person!"

Now no more dragons live in the woods. But in the castle live three brave knights. They are Sir Charles, Sir Egbert, and Sir Olaf!

Their castle is not so big or grand. But they are all very happy.

Monsters of Long Ago

For many years people have told stories about dragons, giants, and other monsters. We do not know who made up the first story about monsters. But we do know that some of the stories are very, very old.

Some of the monsters, like giants and dragons, were very big. Others were as small as cats. But all of the monsters, big or small, could do things that real people or animals could not do.

Many of the old monsters were very mean. People hunted them and tried to kill them. But not all the monsters were bad. In some stories, good monsters worked with people to kill the bad ones.

Many monsters looked like mixed-up animals. Other monsters were part animal and part person. Still others were just giant people, sometimes with two heads!

Here are four of the monsters people told stories about long ago.

This was a friendly monster. It looked like a horse with a man's head. It was a great hunter, for it could run very fast. In one of the old stories, this friendly monster showed people how to do many new things.

You know this monster. It is called a
dragon. It was part bird and part snake.
It had long teeth. Fire came out of its
mouth. In the old tales, most dragons
were very mean. Their cries shook the
woods. They scared people who lived far
away in the cities.

Many of the old stories told how a
brave knight killed a great, bad dragon.

This monster was not friendly at all!
It looked like a lion with a woman's
head. It stopped people who were trying
to go past. It asked them a riddle; then
it killed them if they said the wrong thing.

The old stories said that this monster was part woman and part fish. She lived in the sea, but sometimes came out of the water and sat on the rocks. She liked to sing in the moonlight. In some stories she helped people who were lost at sea.

Should you believe these stories about monsters? No, you should not. People never really saw the monsters they told so many stories about. But they loved to tell monster stories, just as we love to hear them today.

Bigfoot

Many people call the "monster" in this picture Bigfoot. Many people have caught sight of Bigfoot. They say that it looks like a giant monkey. It walks on two feet, as we do. They say that Bigfoot is a head taller than a person. It is as heavy as two large people.

This picture was made in the woods of the American West. "Monsters" that look like Bigfoot have been spotted in many parts of the world.

Study the picture of Bigfoot. Some people say it is the picture of a very big bear. Others feel that it is just a tricky person, having fun in monkey clothes. Still others feel that Bigfoot is a new kind of animal.

Is Bigfoot a real monster? What do you think?

Riddles About Monsters

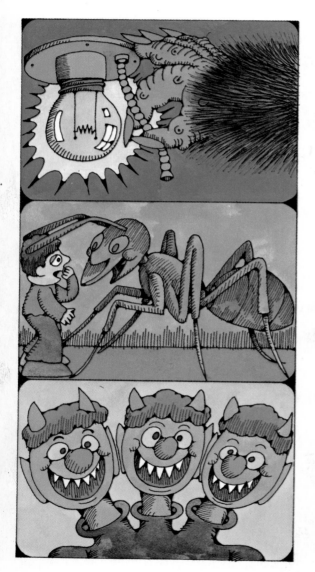

Where were the monsters
when the lights went out?

In the dark.

What are really **big** ants
called?

Giants.

What should you say
when you meet
a three-headed monster?

Hello. Hello. Hello.

28

Monsters in the Schoolroom

Picture Monsters

You can make a monster of your own. You will have lots of fun doing it.

First, find pictures of many kinds of animals. Find some animals that live on land. Find some that fly in the air. Find some that swim in the sea.

When you have the pictures, think what your monster will look like. Take one part from each animal. Try to use as many animal parts as you can.

What kind of head will you give your monster? Will it have a tail? What kind of tail? Will it have legs? How many? Five? Or ten? What about wings?

Now put all the parts together. If your pictures are the right size, cut out the parts. Stick them together on a sheet of paper.

If the pictures are the wrong size, the parts will not fit together. Use your crayons and make a big picture of the monster on a sheet of paper.

Where will your monster live? Will it
live in the deep dark woods? Then cut
out some trees from colored paper. Put
the trees all around your monster.

Should it live in a cave deep in the
mountains? Make a dark cave around it.
Should your monster come from some
other world? Can you make a really
wild home for it?

A Name for Your Monster

It's fun to name your monster. You can make up a name which has never been used before.

If your monster is part fish and part elephant, you might call it **Elefish.**

Or you can just make up a name. This monster is an **Antrog.** That is the name the girl gave it.

Once your monster has a name, sit down and make up a story about it. Tell what magic things your monster has been doing. Then read it to your friends. Will the story be funny? Or will the listeners be filled with fear? Only you can really say, for it is your monster after all!

More Riddles About Monsters

When can you go past a red monster?

When it turns green.

Why is a dragon scared of the dark?

That is when the knight comes.

One monster raced to get away from five dragons. What time was it?

Five after one.

Where Did Dragons Come From?

For years and years, people of many lands have told stories about fearless dragons. They have painted colorful pictures of dragons. They have made dragons out of rock, clay, and wood. They have made toy dragons and masks that look like dragons' heads.

Where did people get their ideas about dragons? Did real dragons once live in the world? Do they still live in the world today?

Look at the picture. It shows animals
that lived long, long ago. Are they dragons?
No, they are not. They are dinosaurs.

Dinosaurs looked a little like dragons.
Some had long teeth and claws. Others
had wings and could fly. But we know
that dinosaurs were not dragons.

We know this because many of the stories about dragons have knights and castles in them. But dinosaurs died out long before there were knights and castles. Besides, many dragons are pictured with fire blowing out of their mouths. No living animal, then or now, can make fire.

So the dragons in books and pictures are not dinosaurs.

An animal that looks a lot like a real dragon is living today. It is a kind of lizard. It is called a dragon lizard.

Some dragon lizards have been caught and sent to city zoos. They are the biggest lizards in the world today. They can grow to be as long as a car!

The dragon lizard has a large red mouth. It has a very long, bright yellow tongue. As the lizard smells around for food, its tongue darts in and out. The tongue looks like a tongue of fire. When the lizard opens its jaws, it shows rows of long teeth. Dragon lizards can be a very fearful sight.

At night a dragon lizard hides in its cave. The cave is one that the lizard makes with its claws.

People's ideas about dragons may have come from dragon lizards. People may have come across dragon lizards in caves. The giant size of the lizard scared them. They may have thought that the lizard's red mouth and yellow tongue were fire. So they told stories about great fearful dragons living in caves.

If that is so, you could say that we do have real dragons in the world today. But these dragons are only a kind of very big lizard.

The Biggest Beast

What is the biggest beast of all?
Is it a giant dark brown bear
Standing in its giant lair?

It's not a bear. A bear is too small
Next to the biggest beast of all.

Elephants are not so small.
Elephants are big and tall.
This is the size that elephants are—
Big as a bus, big as a car,
Big as some boats, and sometimes taller.
All of the other beasts are smaller.

No, not elephants. Elephants are small
Next to the biggest beast of all.

Is it a giant dinosaur?
Some were the size of a house, and more.
Some were so heavy, big, and tall,
I'm sure that they were the biggest of all.

No, dinosaurs are really small
Next to the biggest beast of all.

The biggest beast lives in the sea,
Far away from you and me.
It has no feet and little hair.
It's very large and very rare.
It has no wings, it has no claws.
But it has a mouth with giant jaws,
A giant head, two giant eyes.
It has a fin that is giant-size.
It is a giant, from head to tail.
The biggest beast is . . .

A great Blue Whale
And it is really big!

Jack the Giant Killer

Once upon a time a woman lived on a small farm in Land's End. She had a son named Jack, who was known as a very bright boy.

The people of Land's End would have been happy but for one thing. They lived in fear of a terrible giant.

The giant lived in a big cave in the hills. Each night it came out of its cave. The giant hunted for things to eat. Many a fine cow and many a big sheep did the giant take.

Each morning the people of Land's End talked about the terrible giant. But not one was brave enough to fight the giant.

One night the giant took a sheep from the farm of Jack's mother. The next morning, Jack's mother got up and saw what had happened.

"I wish I were still young," she said. "I would go myself and kill the terrible giant. But I cannot do that. And there are no brave people in Land's End to do it for me."

At that Jack said, "I am brave enough, Mother. I will go out. I will kill the terrible giant this very night."

As soon as it was almost dark, Jack went to the house. He found a shovel and a horn. Then he said good-by to his mother and set out for the hills.

Once there, Jack quietly dug a deep hole at the mouth of the giant's cave. Next he found some long sticks. He put them over the hole. He put grass over the sticks. No one could tell a hole was there.

Then Jack went over to the far side of the hole. He took out his horn and played it very loudly. At once the giant ran to the door of the cave.

"Did you wake me up?" roared the giant. "I'll get you for that. I'll get you and eat you up!"

Jack did not move from the spot. "Come on," he called to the giant. "I'm not scared of you. I have killed many a giant bigger than you."

The giant gave a terrible roar and
raced at Jack. There was a fearful
crash as the giant fell head first into
the deep hole! That was the end of the
terrible giant.

Jack made his way into the giant's
cave. There he saw many bags of gold.
Quickly, Jack ran back to his home.

"Mother," said Jack, "I have killed the giant as you wished. And I have seen its cave. It is filled with gold."

The people of Land's End soon heard the story. They were very happy, for Jack had rid the land of the terrible giant. Jack gave his mother the gold, so that she was very rich. And always after that, the brave boy was known as Jack the Giant Killer.

The Terrible Horrible Giant

Act 1

QUEEN: Eat your eggs, King Egbert.

KING: I'm too tired, Queen Bess. That terrible horrible giant roared all night. I didn't sleep at all.

GIANT (from far away): Ooooh! Oooooh!

(King jumps under a chair.)

QUEEN: Just listen to that terrible horrible noise. Where are you, dear?

KING: I'm here under the chair, Bess.

GIANT: Oooooh! Oooooh!

QUEEN: That noise has to stop. You are the king, so you must do something about it.

(King gets up. Princess runs in.)

PRINCESS: Oh, Mother! Do you hear those terrible horrible noises?

QUEEN: Don't worry, Daughter. Your father will do something about it.

KING: I will? What?

QUEEN: Something! You must think of something, because you are the king.

KING: That's so. All right, quiet, Bess. I am going to think.

(King stands on his head to think, but keeps falling over.)

KING: I have it, I have it!

QUEEN and PRINCESS: What is it?

KING: I'll ask the Wizard to tell me what to do.

PRINCESS: Oh, please don't do that. He gets things mixed up. Once I asked him to make a flying horse for me. Do you know what he made for me? A **crying** horse.

GIANT (very loudly): Ooooooooh!

KING: That noise must stop! Daughter, go get the Wizard.

(Princess goes out of the room.)

KING: Well, what do you think, Bess? Am I acting like a king?

QUEEN: Oh, yes, dear. It always makes me so proud when you do that.

KING: Thank you, Queen Bess.

(The Princess and the Wizard come in. The Wizard carries a book.)

53

PRINCESS: Here is the Wizard.

KING: I need your help, Wizard. A terrible horrible giant is living near here. It makes terrible horrible noises. That has to stop!

WIZARD: A giant, you say? Let me look in the book I'm carrying. Let me see. Giants, big. Giants, small. Oh, here it is. Giants, terrible horrible. "When a terrible horrible giant roars, its noises are terrible and horrible, too."

KING: We know that.

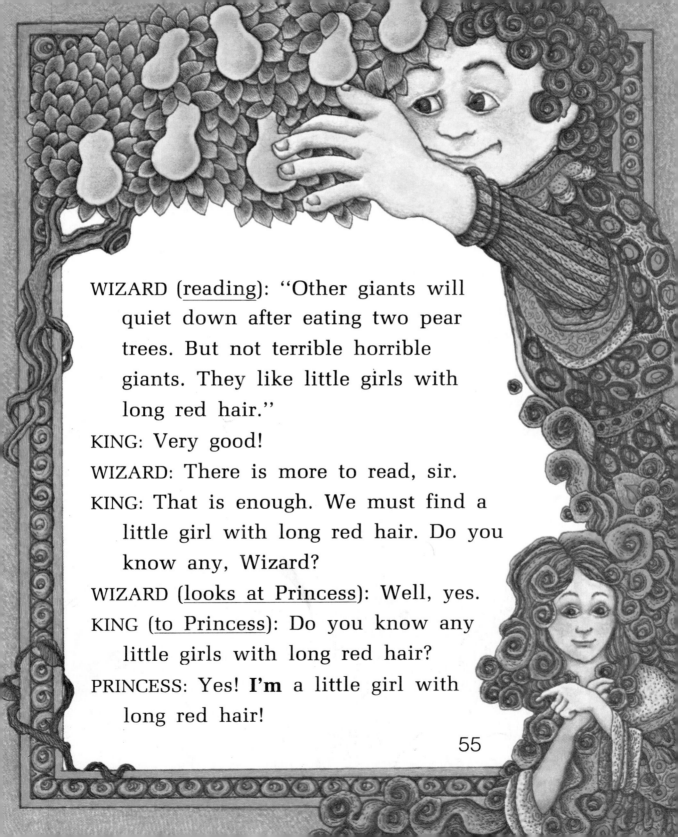

WIZARD (reading): "Other giants will quiet down after eating two pear trees. But not terrible horrible giants. They like little girls with long red hair."

KING: Very good!

WIZARD: There is more to read, sir.

KING: That is enough. We must find a little girl with long red hair. Do you know any, Wizard?

WIZARD (looks at Princess): Well, yes.

KING (to Princess): Do you know any little girls with long red hair?

PRINCESS: Yes! **I'm** a little girl with long red hair!

55

KING: Well, that's fine. I'll have the Princess sent to the giant.

PRINCESS: Don't you dare do that! I know what to do. I'm not scared of the terrible horrible giant. I'll go talk with it.

KING: Then you must go at once!

QUEEN: Are you sure you want to do that, dear?

PRINCESS: Father says I have to.

QUEEN: That's so. Oh, I'm so proud when your father acts like a king!

PRINCESS (leaving): I'm sure that the Wizard's book is wrong. It always is!

End of Act 1

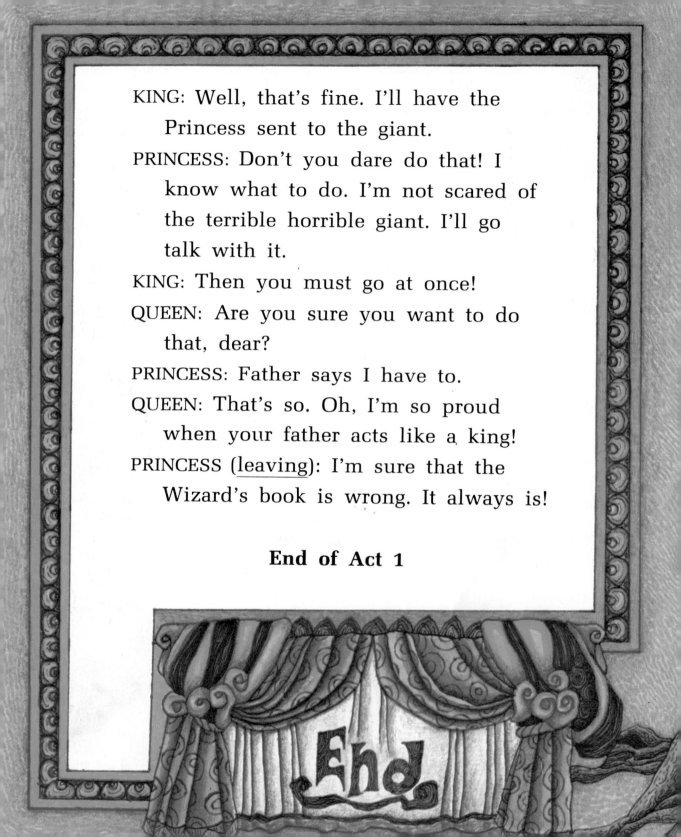

End

The Terrible Horrible Giant

Act 2

(The Princess is in the woods. She sees the Giant.)

GIANT: Ooooh! Oooooh! Poor me!

PRINCESS: I have found you at last. You **are** terrible and horrible.

GIANT: I knew you would say that. Oooooh! Oooooh! Poor me!

PRINCESS: Listen, Giant, you make too much noise. People can't sleep.

57

GIANT: Then all the people must hate me. I'm sure of it. Oh, poor me!

PRINCESS: They don't hate you. They just want you to be quiet. And you must stop eating up people.

GIANT: I never do anything like that!

PRINCESS: Somewhere in the Wizard's book it says that terrible horrible giants like little girls with red hair.

GIANT: That's true. I like all people. But nobody likes me. I'm so lonely.

PRINCESS: Is that why you make those terrible horrible noises?

GIANT: Yes. Oooooh! Poor me. I don't have a friend in the world.

PRINCESS: I will be your friend. You can live in the castle with me.

GIANT: You will? I can?

PRINCESS: **If** you stop making noises.

GIANT: I'll stop, I'll stop!

PRINCESS: Good. Let's go.

(The Princess and Giant walk over
to the King and Queen.)

PRINCESS: I brought a friend to stay
with us.

KING: It's the terrible horrible giant!
Help, he'll eat us all up!

(King jumps under a chair.)

PRINCESS: But this giant likes people.

KING: The Wizard's book says that
giants eat up people.

GIANT (taking book): The book must be
wrong. Please let me read it.
"Terrible horrible giants like little
girls with long red hair."

KING: What did I tell you?

GIANT: There is something else. It says, "Terrible horrible giants like all people. Be kind to them and they will stop making terrible horrible noises."

PRINCESS: What do you say now?

KING: I say that the terrible horrible giant **must** stay with us.

PRINCESS and GIANT: Thank you!

KING (to Queen): Did I do the right thing, Queen Bess?

QUEEN: Oh, yes! I'm always so proud when you act like a king!

What's That Sound?

Some sounds are tricky. They can be spelled in more than one way.

In this poem, listen for words that have the same vowel sound. Look to see if they have the same letters.

Mike the dragon loved to roar,
And did in many places,
Until it made his throat so sore
That now he just makes faces.

<u>Roar</u> and <u>sore</u> have the same vowel sound, but not the same letters. Here are more words like that.

| hair | turn | good |
| scare | bird | would |

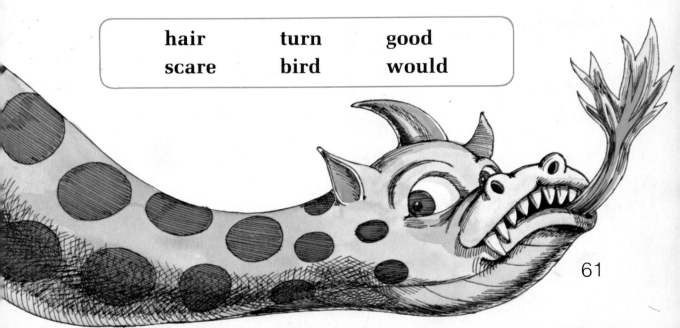

61

Mike the dragon loves to find words that have the same vowel sound. He has found some words in the woods. Listen for the sound that is the same in each set of words. What letters stand for each sound?

burn
first
Egbert

corn
roar
more

lair
pear
dare

Donna the dragon loves words like this, too. She has found two lists of words. Can you help her match the words? Look at the next page. Read each word on the left. Listen for the vowel sound. Then find the words in the list at the right with the same vowel sound.

list 1
jaw
nice
look

list 2
should
fly
caught
kind
brought
walk
light

How many ways did Donna the dragon find to spell each vowel sound?

Some sets of letters don't always stand for the same sound.

"I would like to meet a monster."

"Here, I brought you one."

What letters are the same in would and brought? Do they stand for the same sound in both words?

Read the words in the box and then read the play. Find a word from the box that has the same vowel sound as each underlined word in the play.

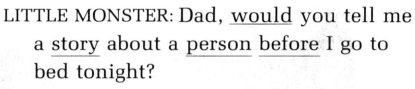

| hair | burn | or | good | caught | night |

LITTLE MONSTER: Dad, <u>would</u> you tell me a <u>story</u> about a <u>person</u> <u>before</u> I go to bed to<u>night</u>?

FATHER MONSTER: Will it <u>scare</u> you?

LITTLE MONSTER: Oh, no!

FATHER MONSTER: <u>All</u> <u>right</u>. Once a <u>girl</u> <u>saw</u> a dragon. "<u>Hi</u>," she said. But the dragon screamed "Good-<u>by</u>!" and ran to its <u>lair</u>. The girl said, "I will go after that dragon."

LITTLE MONSTER: Please stop.

FATHER MONSTER: Why?

LITTLE MONSTER: You were right. The story is scaring me too much!

Surprises

Swing Song

Here I go up in my swing
　　Ever so high.
I am the King of the fields,
　　And the King of the town.
I am the King of the earth,
　　And the King of the sky.
Here I go up in my swing . . .
　　Now I go down.

A. A. MILNE

Martha Matilda O'Toole

by JIM COPP

Martha Matilda O'Toole
Went skipping off to school . . .
But as she turned to go by the gate
Found out that she'd not taken her slate.
Thought Martha, "The teacher won't like
   it a bit.
I'd better go and get it. My, my!"
And she did.

Martha Matilda O'Toole
Went skipping off to school . . .
But an owl saw her coming and hooted, "Oh, look!
Martha Matilda forgot her book!"
    First her slate,
    Then her book,
Martha Matilda forgot her book.
Thought Martha, "The teacher won't like it a bit.
I'd better go get it. My, my!"
And she did.

Martha Matilda O'Toole
Went skipping off to school . . .
But up by the roadside she stopped
    again,
Remembering now that she had no pen.
    First her slate,
    Then her book,
    Then her pen,
Martha Matilda forgot her pen.
Thought Martha, "The teacher won't like
    it a bit.
I'd better go get it. My, my!"
And she did.

Martha Matilda O'Toole
Went skipping off to school . . .
But a blackbird flew past her and said,
   "I have news!
Martha Matilda forgot her shoes!"
   First her slate,
   Then her book,
   Then her pen,
   Then her shoes,
Martha Matilda forgot her shoes.
Thought Martha, "The teacher won't like
   it a bit.
I'd better go get them. My, my!"
And she did.

70

Martha Matilda O'Toole
Went skipping off to school . . .
But when she got there, the teacher
  bowed low.
"The school isn't open. It's Sunday, you
  know."
"If that is the rule," said Martha, "I'll sit
And wait for tomorrow. Oh, dear."
And she did.

Mrs. Simkin's Bed

by LINDA ALLEN

"Stanley," said Mrs. Simkin to Mr. Simkin one day. "There's a pig under the bed."

"What color is it?" asked Mr. Simkin.

Mrs. Simkin looked again.

"It's a pink one," she said.

"Then we must find out who owns it," said Mr. Simkin. "We can't have a pink pig under the bed."

Mr. Simkin went to ask his friend if he had lost a pink pig.

"No," said his friend. "I lost twenty-four cans of soup once, on a bus. But I have never lost a pink pig."

"Then it can't be yours," said Mr. Simkin.

Mrs. Simkin talked about it to the woman next door. The woman next door said she would be buying a small gray horse in the next few weeks.

Mr. Robinson, who lived across the street, said he had a water buffalo in his greenhouse.

"Stanley," said Mrs. Simkin. "I really think we will have to keep the little pink pig. Your friend doesn't own it. The woman next door doesn't want it. And Mr. Robinson has a water buffalo. What else can we do?"

"But what can we call it?" asked Mr. Simkin.

"Marcia," said Mrs. Simkin. "That's a nice name for a pig."

So they bought a little blue bonnet for Marcia and a ladder for when she wanted to climb the pear tree.

Marcia was a very nice little pig. She never sat in the flowerpots, or painted pictures on the back door, or anything like that. Mr. Simkin and Mrs. Simkin liked Marcia very much.

Mr. Simkin made her a pen to sit in. Marcia was very happy.

On Mr. Simkin's birthday Mrs. Simkin said to him, "Stanley, there's another pig under the bed."

"Is it another pink one?" asked Mr. Simkin.

"Yes," said Mrs. Simkin.

"Well, she can sit in the pen with Marcia," said Mr. Simkin.

So they named the new little pig Veronica, after the woman next door. Veronica sat in the pen with Marcia, and they had long talks together.

Mr. Simkin went to see his friend again. "You still haven't lost a pink pig, have you?" he asked.

"No," said his friend. "And I still haven't found my twenty-four cans of soup."

"Never fear," said Mr. Simkin. "You're sure to find them one day."

Mrs. Simkin found another pink pig under the bed the following day. She found another one on the day that her young friend Ann won a prize for jumping over a yellow wagon.

Mrs. Simkin found a lot of pink pigs. "Each time I look under the bed I find another pink pig there," she said to Mr. Simkin.

Soon they had forty-seven pink pigs.

The pen was filled with little pink pigs. There were no more blue bonnets in town. And Mr. Simkin had to climb over all the ladders when he wanted to go out.

"It's not that I don't like pink pigs," he said to Mrs. Simkin one day. "But they do get in one's way now and then. Should we give some of them away?"

"Oh, no, Stanley," said Mrs. Simkin. "That would never do."

"Then there's only one thing to do," said Mr. Simkin. "We'll have to sell the bed."

"Sell the bed!" cried Mrs. Simkin.

"It's the only way," Mr. Simkin said.

Mrs. Simkin was sad.

"Do you want to buy a bed?" Mr. Simkin asked a man in the park.

"Oh, yes!" he said. "Why do you want to sell it?"

"We keep finding pink pigs under it," said Mr. Simkin.

"I don't care about that," said the man.

He went to the house with Mr.
Simkin and looked at the bed. "It's a
very nice bed," he said. And he took
the bed away.

Mrs. Simkin bought a new bed. It
was a beautiful bed. It had large gold
flowers on it. There were no pink pigs
under it.

Mr. Simkin and Mrs. Simkin and the forty-seven pink pigs were very happy living all together.

Mrs. Simkin used to look under the new bed each day.

"Stanley," said Mrs. Simkin one morning. "Isn't it odd? There's a pig under the new bed."

"What!" cried Mr. Simkin. "Our new bed! Another pink pig?"

Mrs. Simkin shook her head. "Oh, no, dear," she said. "This is a black one."

Mr. Simkin smiled happily. "That's all right then," he said.

The White Kite

by RAY SIPHERD

At the Park

Pablo liked to make up stories.

One morning he saw a cat near the window. He told his mother a long story about a great lion that was living outside the house.

Once Pablo got a little rock in his shoe. He told his friends that it was a piece of gold.

Near Pablo's school was a park. Late one afternoon he saw five girls flying kites in the park. The kites looked like birds and fish and dragons. They were almost as high as the clouds. As Pablo watched, the girls made their kites do tricks. If he had a kite, Pablo was sure he'd make it do tricks, too.

Then some girls came running, pulling on kite strings. Pablo saw a giant blue kite. It blew right past and shot into the air.

"What a big kite!" Pablo said.

"The biggest one here," said the girl.

"Can I fly it?" Pablo asked.

"Sure," the girl said.

She gave the string to Pablo. "Now run with it," she said.

Pablo let out the string as he ran. The kite blew higher and higher.

At last the girl said, "I'd like my kite back now." So Pablo handed her the string. The girl ran off.

There were many tall old trees in the park. Pablo walked along, looking up into the branches. All at once he stopped at the foot of a large tree. Something was high in the leaves of the tree. It was a kite string. Quickly Pablo climbed the tree. Soon he was up to the very top branches. There in the branches was the kite string. And it went above the tree up into the sky.

83

Slowly Pablo shook the string out of the leaves. Then he climbed down from the tree. He looked up. The sky was filled with kites of many colors. Pablo gave the string a pull. But not one of the kites moved.

Then Pablo looked above the kites.

He saw the moon. He shook the string again. The moon moved!

Pablo could not believe his eyes. Slowly he pulled down on the string once more. Slowly the moon came down.

"I caught the moon!" Pablo shouted. "My string goes up to the moon!"

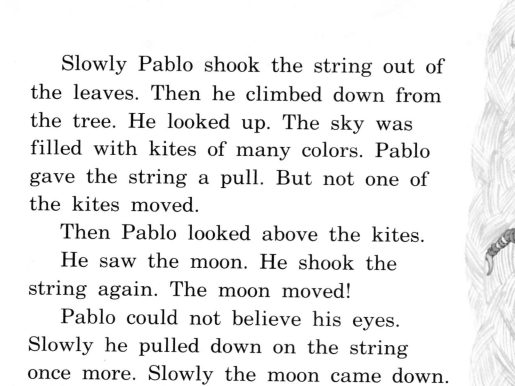

Soon it got dark. Pablo hid the kite string in the tree and ran home. He told Father that he'd found a string that went up to the moon.

"A string that goes to the moon?" laughed Father.

And I can fly the moon like a kite!" said Pablo.

"What a wild idea!" said Father. "The moon is a giant ball of rock many miles away. It couldn't be on a string."

"But if it were?" Pablo asked.

"It isn't, Pablo," said Father.

Magic Moon

Late the next day, Pablo went
back to the tree in the park. He took
down the string and flew the moon
again. Soon he had taught the moon
to do tricks.

Each day the moon was higher
in the sky. The string pulled harder
in Pablo's hands.

One day Pablo saw some children
nearby. "See what my kite can do!"
he called.

The children looked up into the sky.
"Where is it?" they asked.

"It's—the white kite," Pablo said.

"I don't see any white kite," said
a girl.

"You don't have a kite at all!" said
a boy.

"But I do!" Pablo told them. "My
kite is the moon! And I can make the
moon do tricks! Look!"

He shook the kite string and waited. But the moon didn't move.

Carrying the string above his head, Pablo ran and jumped. He ran and jumped again. But the moon just sat in the sky.

The children laughed. "Fly the moon? Make the moon do tricks? No one can do that!" a girl said as they ran off.

Pablo looked up at the moon. He said, "Did I fly the moon? Did I make the moon do tricks?"

All at once the string pulled very hard. Before Pablo knew it, he was high up in the air. He looked down and saw that he was flying over trees, roofs, and water towers.

Pablo saw a pool of water. If he let go of the string, he'd fall into the water. So Pablo shut his eyes and let go. Down and down he went. He fell with a loud SPLASH into the pool.

"Pablo, look at you! You're all wet!"
Mother said when he came home.
"What have you been doing?"

"I was playing," Pablo said to her.

"Playing where?" Mother asked.

"In the park," he said.

Pablo knew that Mother would not
believe the story about the moon. So
he told her, "I was playing in the
park, and I fell into a pool of water."

Mother laughed. "I thought you'd
tell me one of your stories," she said.

Pablo didn't say a thing.

That night, Pablo was in his bed,
thinking about the moon. He thought
about the day he'd found the kite
string in the tree. He thought about
the tricks he'd taught the moon. He
thought about the ride the moon had
given him that day.

Slowly, light started to come in the
window of his room. Slowly it grew
brighter. Pablo saw that the moon was
shining high above. It was round and
white. He was sure he saw a kite
string, too, as the moon moved higher
in the sky.

I'm up here.
You're down there.
And nothing in that
    space between us
But a mile of air.
Where I sail:
Clouds pass.
Where you run:
Green grass.
Where I float:
Birds sing.
One thin thing there is
That holds us together:
Kite string.

KARLA KUSKIN

What's It All About?

Don had just read a story.
"What was it about?" Jill asked.
Don thought hard. Then he said, "It was about some people who were always finding pigs under the bed."

Don told Jill the main idea of the story. He told her what the story was about. He did not tell all the things that went on in the story.

Finding the main idea in a story or book helps you to understand and remember what you read. Ask yourself, "What was the story about?"

What is the main idea of this story?

Waking Up Harry

"Wake up, Harry," called Father.

"Wake up, Harry!" called Mother.

Harry did not wake up.

"WAKE UP, HARRY!" called all the neighbors.

Still Harry did not wake up.

Harry did not want to wake up until he had a good reason.

Then Carla came in. She said softly, "Come, we have to get ready for Besty's birthday party, Harry."

Harry opened his eyes and smiled.

"Good morning, everyone," he said.

Was your main idea something like this? Harry did not want to wake up until he had a good reason.

94

Jill was reading a book about making things. Here is one part of the book.

You need different things to make your own kite. You'll need two long, thin pieces of wood, a big sheet of paper, glue, and a lot of string. You will also need tools for cutting the paper and the wood.

If you were asked to tell the main idea, you might say something like this. "You need different things to make your own kite."

But what if a friend asked you, "Well, what <u>do</u> you need to make a kite?" You'd have to tell more than the main idea. You would have to tell the details. Which details in Jill's book tell more about the main idea?

Turn back to page 29 and read it.
- What is the main idea of what you read?
- What are the details that tell you more about the main idea?

Can I? I Can!

The Big Dipper

by PHYLLIS KRASILOVSKY

Benny lived in Alaska many years before it was a state. He had black hair and bright black eyes. He always had a happy, friendly smile.

Everyone liked Benny. He had many, many friends in the home where he lived. Benny was happy in the home. But sometimes before going to sleep at night, he would look at the stars outside the window. He would long for the day when he could be a grown-up. For then he was going to be a fine fisherman.

Benny looked at the Big Dipper. He knew it was part of the Great Bear of the night sky. He found the North Star, the star that did not move in the sky. One day, when Benny was a fisherman, he would use the North Star to help bring the boat safely back to land at night. Benny knew that the North Star was the star of Alaska.

One day a kind fisherman took Benny fishing in a boat. Almost at once Benny caught a big fish. Benny was so happy he could not sleep that night. He looked out the window at the stars. He thought about being a real fisherman one day.

One day at school the teacher told the children about a contest.

"Alaska does not have a flag," she said. "So we are holding a contest. Children from all over Alaska are making pictures of flags. The best picture will be made into Alaska's flag."

Benny wanted very much to do well in the contest. He thought how grand it would be to see his flag in a parade. He thought how grand it would be to see his flag flying on the fishing boat he would have one day.

That night Benny sat quietly, thinking about the flag. He thought of what he loved most about Alaska. All at once, Benny knew what the flag must look like. He wanted the flag to be like the stars he loved—gold stars like the Big Dipper in the dark blue sky. So that is what he painted.

Under the picture he put, "The North Star is for the state of Alaska. The Big Dipper is for the Great Bear—standing for a strong state."

Benny didn't show the paper to his friends. The next day, he gave it to the teacher.

Many days went by, and the teacher
did not say a thing about the contest
again. Benny skated and played in the
snow with the other children.

Then, one day, when school was
almost over, the teacher called the
children together. "Children," she said,
"the flag contest is over. From all over
Alaska boys and girls have sent in
pictures for the flag. And . . . boys
and girls! Benny's picture was the best!
From now on, Benny's picture will be
Alaska's flag."

How proud and happy Benny was!
And how very proud he was on the
Fourth of July. On that day there was
a big parade. People came from all
over Alaska to see it.

The very first thing they saw was
Benny. Benny was walking at the head
of the parade. In his hands was the
flag he had made for the fishing boat he
would have one day. It was the flag he
had made for Alaska.

THE PAINTED HOUSE

Father was smiling. He was having the best time painting the house. He wasn't painting it plain white, the way it always had been.

"Next, I'll paint a band of blue for the sky," he said. "Then, I'll make big splashes of gray for the clouds. And then some green mountains. Maybe I'll paint silly pictures all over the house."

Before long, Mother came out of the house. She started laughing when she saw what was going on.

"Our house will be odd-looking," she said. "But what fun we'll have painting it. What should I paint?"

She bent down and painted a bright blue sea. Then she painted some white whales and yellow boats. She put a monkey on one of the boats.

Mother and Father were laughing and having a great time. But then the children came home from school.

"What's going on?" asked Jill when she saw the house. "All our friends will laugh at us."

"Why are you acting so silly?" asked Herbert.

"Take it easy, children," said Mother. "I'll tell you about it. In a way it's bad news. The city needs land to build a new school. They are going to buy our lot, pull down our house, and build a bigger school right here. So you see, we have to move."

At first, Jill and Herbert were quiet. Then Jill said, "But we have always lived here. We don't want to move."

"I like living here," Herbert said. "It's next to our school, so we're never late."

"Where will we live?" Jill asked.

"Not far away," Mother said. "And our new house will be bigger."

"That's good," said Jill. "We need a bigger house now that Grandmother lives with us."

"I still don't get it," said Herbert.
"Why are you painting our house if it's
going to be pulled down?"

"Just to have some fun," said Mother.
"People always use plain colors on
houses. We got sick of the same old
thing. So we are doing something
different. Come on, you can help."

"Great!" Jill cried. "Can we paint any
pictures we want?"

"Sure," said Father. "Just have fun."

Soon, the children were painting the house, too. Jill painted a green horse and a box of treasure. Herbert painted a blue dinosaur and big flowers all along the window frames.

Father painted a giant doorknob and key over the doorbell. Mother painted red buses and blue trains filled with odd animals.

108

Grandmother came out and helped, too. She was very proud of her buffalo. Before night, there were bright pictures all over the outside of the house.

"We don't care how odd our house looks," Grandmother said. "The bulldozers will be pushing it down soon."

Days went by, but no bulldozers came. Then, one day, a letter came.

When Father read the letter, he cried, "Oh, no! I'm afraid we won't be moving. They're not going to buy our lot after all. Now they plan to build the school on River Street."

"I can't believe it!" Mother said.

But the children were very happy. They didn't have to move!

As for Mother and Father, it was a good thing they liked to paint, because now they had to paint the house all over again. And this time, no one wanted to help. After all, what fun is it to paint a house plain white?

The One-Dollar Problem

by DINA ANASTASIO

It was a hot summer afternoon, and Carla was playing ball in front of her building. All at once, the sky darkened and great sheets of rain started to fall. Carla caught the ball and ran up on her porch.

As she stood watching the rain, Mr. Norton, her next-door neighbor, hurried out of the rain. He stood beside her.

"The rains have come, Carla," he said. "And they caught me by surprise!"

Just then, a boy hurried up to the porch. "I didn't think it would come down so hard," he said. "This is really some rain!"

Then a girl opened the door of the building. She walked over to them, stood beside Carla, and watched the rain.

After a time, Carla looked down. She saw a dollar bill by her shoe. She picked it up. It crackled in her hand.

"I believe that the dollar is mine, Carla," said Mr. Norton.

The boy took a dollar from his pocket. "It can't be," said the boy. "I had two dollars, and now I only have one. So it has to be mine."

The girl said, "No, it's mine. My mother just gave it to me."

Carla looked at the three people. She thought, "All three of them really believe the dollar is theirs."

She said, "All of you think you own this dollar. But two of you must be wrong. Why don't you each tell me your story? Then I'll try to tell who should have this dollar."

"I'll do that," said Mr. Norton.

Mr. Norton's Story

"I was sitting outside at the snack bar, getting something to eat. I called the owner and gave her some money. She gave me some money back. She put it down on the table. Then, it started to rain.

"The rain caught me by surprise, as you can see. I jumped up, put the money in my pocket, and ran here. Now I cannot find one of the dollars. So that dollar must be mine."

The Boy's Story

"I went swimming this afternoon," said the boy. "Before I jumped into the pond, I took two dollars out of my pocket. I did not want them to get wet. I put a rock on top of them so that they would not blow away. When it started to rain, I jumped out of the pond, picked them up, and put them in my pocket. Then I jumped on my bicycle and hurried here. Now I have only one dollar. So the dollar has to be mine."

The Girl's Story

The girl said, "I was inside, playing, when my mother said, 'Maria, we need some bread. Please take this dollar and run to the store.' Just as I came to the door, it started to rain. So I came out and watched it with you. Then I saw that the dollar was lost. So that dollar must be mine. That is my story."

Carla listened to the stories. Then the three waited as Carla thought about the problem. First, she moved the dollar from her left hand to her right hand. As she moved the dollar, it crackled.

Carla smiled. "I know who owns this dollar," she said.

Carla turned and handed the dollar to the girl. "It's yours, Maria," she said.

"No, it's mine!" said the boy.

"You must have left your dollar at the pond," said Carla.

"It's mine!" said Mr. Norton.

"I think you left your dollar on the snack bar table," said Carla.

"How do you know that?" asked Mr. Norton and the boy at the same time.

Carla told them. And they knew that the dollar was Maria's.

What did Carla tell them?

Mr. Norton's dollar and the boy's dollar had been out in the rain. A wet dollar bill does not "crackle." So the only one who could have had a dry dollar that "crackled" was the one who had not been in the rain.—Maria.

117

The Storm

It was a stormy afternoon. Rain fell and splashed on the streets and lawns. The wind screamed, and low gray clouds raced across the sky.

Two children, Nell and Joshua, were walking by the park. School was over, and they were on their way home.

Nell's yellow coat floated up in the wind, and the cold rain fell from her hair. Joshua had on a black raincoat and a black rainhat that made him look like a firefighter. They were walking into the wind, heads low, and they did not talk. Then Nell saw the little cat.

The cat had crawled under a tree, but it was not out of the storm. Its gray fur was very wet. It had put its head on its paws and closed its eyes.

The children stopped and looked at the cat.

"Is it O.K., Nell?" Joshua asked.

"I think so," said Nell. "Let's go and see."

Slowly, the children walked up to the cat. Then they heard it—it was meowing softly, as if it were singing to the storm.

"Poor cat!" said Nell, "Oh, you poor thing!"

The cat opened its eyes and looked at them. Its eyes were large and sad; but as the children watched, the eyes filled with fear. The cat tried to jump away from them. It could not. The wind caught it and pushed it back to the ground.

Joshua got down by the cat. He opened his raincoat over it. "Poor cat, don't be scared," he said softly. "Don't be scared." He talked quietly until he had gentled the cat.

Slowly, the fear left the cat's eyes. It meowed softly.

Nell bent down and petted it. She petted the cat hard, pushing the water out of its fur. The cat's back went up under her hand.

"The poor wet thing," Nell said. "What can we do with it?"

"Let's take it home," said Joshua.

"We can't do that," said Nell. "Dad can't stand animals in the house."

"We can't just leave it here," said Joshua. "We have to do something."

Nell looked up into the rain. She knew that the storm would not let up for a long time.

"O.K., we can try," she said. "Here, give it to me." She picked the cat up. Its fur was really wet. Nell wanted to hold the cat under her coat, but she did not dare get her clothes wet. So she held the cat as close as she could. The cat was small and light. It rested its head on her raincoat, and Nell put her hand over its ears.

"Here." Joshua took off his rainhat and gave it to Nell.

"Joshua, you'll get all wet. What will Dad say?"

"Let me worry about that," said Joshua. "Use it, Nell."

Nell put the black rainhat around the cat. Now the cat was safe from the wind and rain. The children bent their heads and walked slowly out of the park. When they were near their house, Nell stopped. "Come here, Joshua, listen," she said.

Joshua bent and listened. Then he smiled. The cat's eyes were closed, and it was purring.

When they got to the house, Father was waiting at the door. "Where have you been?" he asked. "I was worried. Joshua, where is your hat?"

Then he saw the cat. "Nell, put that animal down," he said.

"Oh, no," said Nell, "please!"

"No, no animals in this house!" said Father. "Put it down and come in, you two. It's a terrible storm, and you should be glad to be home."

Slowly, Nell pulled the cat away from her. It did not want to leave. Its claws held gently to Nell's coat and then let go. Nell put the cat down on the steps. The cat looked around. It was still purring.

"Inside," said Father.

Joshua started to cry. Father looked at him in surprise. Joshua **never** cried. "Just for now," said Joshua, "just until it stops raining."

Father looked at Joshua. His hair was wet with the cold rain. He looked at Nell. She stood quiet, small, and sad. Then he looked out at the street. It was dark now, but sheets of rain were falling near the street lights. He could hear the screaming wind and feel the cold.

"You're right, children," he said at last. "We have room in our house for it. The cat can stay with us until the storm is over."

"Oh, thank you!" said Nell. She picked up the cat again. This time, she opened her coat and held the cat inside. Then she followed Joshua and Father into the house.

That night, the storm went on and on. The wind blew and rain fell in rivers from the roof to the lawn. But the storm only made the house seem smaller and closer. That night, the storm crashed and screamed. But Father, Nell, Joshua, and the cat felt very happy and very safe.

What Do You Think?

Read this story and then tell what you think Rosa should do.

Rosa was going to be late for school. She raced to the door. Once she was outside, she remembered something.

"Oh, no!" she cried. "I left all of my books in my room. I need them for school today. I had better go back and get them. No, I can't do that. That will make me even later for school!"

What should Rosa do?

At times it is hard to say what a person should do. Think about Rosa's problem. Is it better to be a little late and not have your schoolbooks? Or is it better to be later and have your schoolbooks? What would you do?

Read the next part of Rosa's story. Think about what Rosa should do.

Rosa ran down the street. Maybe she would not be late for school after all. She was just across the street from the school. Oh, no! The light had just turned red. There were no cars in the street, and Rosa heard the schoolbell start to ring. What should she do?

One morning, Bob asked Sara if he could go to her house. He wanted to play with some of the new games she had.

"Sure, come over," said Sara.

"Great," said Bob. "I'll come to your house this afternoon."

But late that morning, it started to rain. It rained hard.

Bob said, "I really want to go to Sara's house. But she lives all the way over on Green Street. I don't want to walk all that way and get wet in the rain."

What should Bob do? What would you do?

Sleep is good for you. Does that mean that sleeping all the time is very good for you? Why not? Tell what you think.

Going Places

The First Hot-Air Balloon

by DINA ANASTASIO

Have you ever had a dream that would not go away? A dream that stayed with you and stayed with you? It might have been a small dream, like wanting some very nice shoes. Or it might have been a big dream, like hitting three home runs in one game.

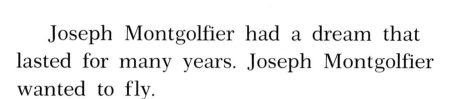

Joseph Montgolfier had a dream that lasted for many years. Joseph Montgolfier wanted to fly.

But there was one problem. Joseph lived in the 1700's, long before there were any planes.

Joseph tried and tried to think of a way to fly. At first, he sat and looked at the birds. He wanted to know what made them fly. Then, when he was still young, he made a parachute and jumped off the roof of a tall building. This was fun, but it wasn't really flying. It was only floating down to the ground.

He said, "A bird doesn't just go down. It also goes up. If I'm going to fly like a bird, I'll have to find a way to go up."

The dream stayed with Joseph for more than twenty-five years. It was there as he sat in school. It was there when he talked to friends. He was always thinking about how to make the dream come true.

Then one day he sat in front of the fire and looked at the smoke. It floated up from the logs.

"Why does the smoke go up?" he asked. "Why?"

Then all at once, he knew! The smoke was lighter than the air around it! At last Joseph had the answer.

Quickly, he found a bag and put it over the fire. The bag floated up into the air. Joseph ran to find his brother.

"I've found it! I've found it!" he shouted happily.

"Found what?" asked his brother.

"The answer," Joseph said. "Hot air is lighter than cold air. So it can float up, the way smoke floats up. It's as easy as that. I think we're going to fly at last."

It was a long way from a cloth bag to a ride in a balloon. It took many more years before Joseph and his brother could really fly.

First they made a bigger bag. Then they made a small fire outside their house. They filled the bag with heated air. Again, the bag went up. But it didn't go very high.

"We need a bigger bag," they said.

The next bag was bigger. It went higher. But it still didn't go as high as they wanted.

So they made bigger and bigger bags that went higher and higher. At last they made one that could go high up into the sky. It was called a hot-air balloon.

The brothers put a small basket under the balloon. They put a rooster, a duck, and a sheep in the basket. They made a fire on the ground and heated the air in the balloon. Then they let the balloon go.

The balloon floated high up into the sky. When it landed, the animals looked as if they had liked the ride very much.

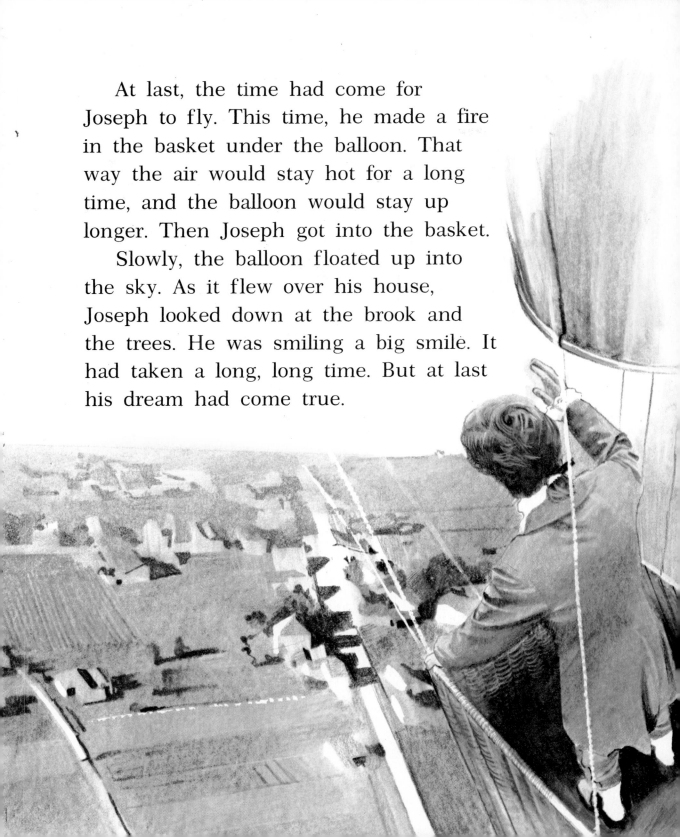

At last, the time had come for
Joseph to fly. This time, he made a fire
in the basket under the balloon. That
way the air would stay hot for a long
time, and the balloon would stay up
longer. Then Joseph got into the basket.

Slowly, the balloon floated up into
the sky. As it flew over his house,
Joseph looked down at the brook and
the trees. He was smiling a big smile. It
had taken a long, long time. But at last
his dream had come true.

The Flying Shoes

by CYNTHIA JAMESON

Long, long ago, there lived an old man who walked as fast as the wind.

Each year he would come down from the hills to the village. On his back he carried great bags filled with rare plants. These he would bring to the village to trade for a few eggs and corn. He never said a thing. He would come and go, softly and quietly, like a cloud passing over the sun.

One fine summer day, the old man went down to the village. When he had traded all his plants, he set out on the long walk back to the hills. He stopped to rest under some tall trees. He sat on the grass and listened to the sounds of the woods.

Soon a girl came walking up the road.

"Old father," she said. "Let me sit by you and rest my feet. I must carry this wood to my master. And the road is very rough."

"My daughter," said the old man, "I am not surprised that your feet hurt. For your shoes are nothing but holes."

The girl looked at the old man's fine shoes. Her eyes lighted up. As if reading the girl's thoughts, the old man said quickly, "Oh, no. My shoes are not new. They are almost as old as I am."

At this, the girl's eyes grew big with surprise.

"I made them myself when I was young," the old man went on. "And I have always taken good care of them. I call them my flying shoes. They carry me all over the world as fast as the wind."

"These are the very shoes I need!" thought the girl. "Let the old one make himself some new shoes. I will take these as soon as I can."

She did not have long to wait. The bright sun and the buzzing of the bees soon put the old one to sleep.

Quickly the girl took off the shoes. She put her own on the old one's feet. Then she put on the flying shoes.

But no sooner had she done this than
the girl raced up the road. She could
not stop!

All at once she was flying over the
houses and people. She had raced past
the village like the wind. At last, she
turned herself about. She headed back to
the village where her master lived. Alas!
The shoes had a will of their own!

The girl found herself falling! Her
legs kicked wildly over her head. Children
from all over the village came running
to see the odd sight.

"Help!" the girl cried wildly. "My
shoes! Pull them off!"

Quickly the children jumped upon her legs. They pulled and pulled until one shoe—then the other—popped off.

The girl got up. Then, carrying the flying shoes in her hands, she ran to the house of her master.

When she got there, she saw that the house was filled with people.

The master ran up to her. "Where have you been with the wood?" he roared. "We are waiting for our supper!"

He was about to hit the girl when he saw her shoes.

"What beautiful shoes!" he thought. "How did the girl come by them? If only they were mine!"

Then an idea came to the master. He would just say that the shoes were his!

And so he said roughly, "Girl, bring the shoes I bought this morning. I wish to put them on."

The girl was so scared that she could not move. "But, master . . ." she said.

"Bring them here, I say!" shouted the master. At this, all heads turned to see what the shouting was all about. Slowly the girl set the flying shoes before her master.

How the people loved the shoes! They said, "See the shoes he has bought! How beautiful they are! He must be very rich!"

This pleased the master very much. He smiled as he put his feet into the shoes. But, alas! No sooner had he done that than he jumped up and started a wild dance. Madly he whirled about, jumping over chairs and hopping up and down in the air.

The people thought this was all in
fun. They stamped their feet and
shouted. And the more noise they made,
the faster the man whirled around.

"Stop me!" he cried. "The shoes!
They have a will of their own!"

The people ran after him, trying to catch him by holding onto his clothes. And now the master whirled out the door, into the street.

Before anyone could get to the man, he made a high jump. He was caught on the branch of a tree. There he stayed, kicking and shouting, as the people tried to get the flying shoes.

"Get your shoes off me! I don't want them!" the master cried to the girl. The girl ran up to the tree and pulled hard at the shoes.

Off came one — then the other.

"I don't want these shoes," said the girl. "They have a will of their own." She threw the shoes high into the air.

At first the flying shoes flew around and around in the sky. Then they darted down into the shadows of some tall trees.

Under one tall tree was an old man.

His shoes were nothing but holes. The
flying shoes fell to the ground. And the
old one opened his eyes.

Slowly he picked up one — then the
other. Then with a knowing smile, he
took off the old shoes and put on his
own flying shoes.

And now, once more he set off, as
fast as the wind, on the long walk back
to his home in the hills.

Wind on the Hill

No one can tell me,
   Nobody knows,
Where the wind comes from,
   Where the wind goes.

It's flying from somewhere
   As fast as it can,
I couldn't keep up with it,
   Not if I ran.

But if I stopped holding
   The string of my kite
It would blow with the wind
   For a day and a night.

148

And then when I found it,
    Wherever it blew,
I should know that the wind
    Had been going there too.

So then I could tell them
    Where the wind goes . . .
But where the wind comes from
    Nobody knows.

A. A. MILNE

Whirlybirds at Work

Have you ever seen a helicopter
take off? Its metal blades start to turn.
They turn faster and faster. Then the
helicopter goes straight up into the air.

Once a helicopter is in the air, it
can fly near the ground or high above
it. It can fly fast or very slow. It can
fly sideways. It can stop safely at one
spot in the air and then turn all the
way around!

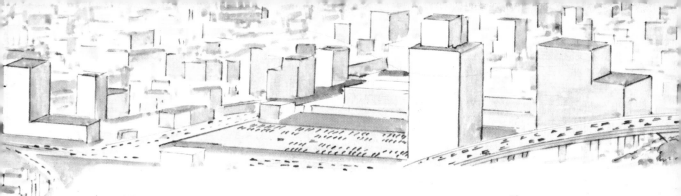

The people who fly helicopters sometimes call them "whirlybirds." Can you tell why?

Many cities find helicopters useful in keeping traffic moving. In this picture you see a helicopter police officer. She is flying over the city. From high up, she can see where traffic is stopped and where it is moving freely.

If she spots something wrong, she reports it at once. Other police officers are then sent out to help people who are hurt and to keep the traffic moving safely.

Helicopter traffic reports are very helpful to drivers. The reports help them pick the best way to get around the city.

Helicopters go up and down. They stay in one place in the air. So helicopters are very helpful to people who are making a tall building.

Large building parts are put under the helicopter. Up it goes, carrying the parts. Then it stops in the air, and people put the parts in place. The helicopter goes down for more parts. It goes up and down, up and down, until the building is done.

Today, some cowboys in the West no longer ride horses. They ride in whirlybirds. They use helicopters to look for lost animals. And when it's round-up time, cowboys herd the animals together by flying over them in helicopters.

In wintertime, farm animals can get lost in the deep snow. They are far from farmhouses. They may not find enough to eat. But cowboys can carry food to them—in whirlybirds!

The picture shows a person in the water. He will drown unless help comes quickly.

But the man is lucky. A whirlybird is floating in the air above him. It will pull the helpless man up out of the water and he will be safe.

A helicopter cannot fly as fast or as far as a big plane. Most helicopters cannot carry as many people as a train or a city bus. But in some ways helicopters are more useful than planes, trains, or city buses. Many times, using a helicopter is the best way to do a job. Sometimes it is the only way.

Racing on the Wind

by E. and R. S. RADLAUER

Think about the wind. It cools us when we are hot. It moves the flowers and the leaves in trees. It makes waves on lakes. But the wind can be fun as well. All around the world, people use the wind to sail, to fly, and to race.

Here are four ways that people use the wind to have great fun.

Land Sailing

When people say, "We're going sailing," what do you think of? Do you think that they will be sailing on a boat in the water? You could be wrong.

There are other kinds of sailing. Land sailing is one.

A land sailor drives a small car that has three wheels and a sail. The sailor turns it by moving the sail. The front wheel is sometimes used for turning, and it helps the sailor to stop, too.

Most land-sailing races take place on hot sand or on lakes that dried up long ago. Drivers like these places because they are flat, there is a lot of room, and the wind blows very hard.

There are different kinds of land-sailing contests. In some, the drivers try to go as fast as they can. The cars are very light and can go much faster than a boat in water. In other races, the drivers try to sail around markers placed on the ground. They try not to touch any of the markers.

Iceboat Sailing

Iceboat sailing uses the wind, too.
An iceboat has no wheels. It has
runners, like a sled. Iceboat racing is
very cold, because it must take place on
a lake that has ice as hard as a rock.

Most iceboat races use markers that have been placed on the ice. Drivers sail around the markers. They turn the boat by pulling a rope that moves the sail. The driver can move the boat to the left or the right by leaning out of the boat. When the wind is in back of the driver, an iceboat can go very, very fast.

Gliders

Have you ever looked up on a hot summer day and seen a glider riding the wind? Did you know how it stayed in the air?

A glider is like a large, very well-made paper plane. If things are just right, it can stay in the air for a long, long time.

To take off, a glider pilot may roll down a steep hill. Other glider pilots get up in the air with the help of a plane. When the glider and plane are in the air, the pilot of the glider unhooks the rope. Then the glider is on its own.

Glider pilots stay up in the sky by finding air that is going up. This air pushes up on the glider's wings and keeps the plane in the air.

Glider pilots stay up as long as they can find the right kind of air. Sometimes this is not very long. But there are places in the world where they can stay up all day.

Hot–Air Balloons

When there is very little wind, it's hot-air balloon time. Putting a balloon into the air takes a lot of work.

First, the balloon is placed on the ground. Next, the balloon is filled with air. The air in the balloon is then heated with a burner.

Balloon riders sit in a small basket under the balloon. This basket also carries the burner that is used to heat the air in the balloon. The ride in a hot-air balloon can be very quiet. You are moving just as fast as the wind, so you cannot hear it or feel it.

Balloon riders do not like rough winds. Rough winds can break up their balloon. But when the wind is right, balloon riders, like other riders of the wind, have lots of fun.

Racing
on the Ice

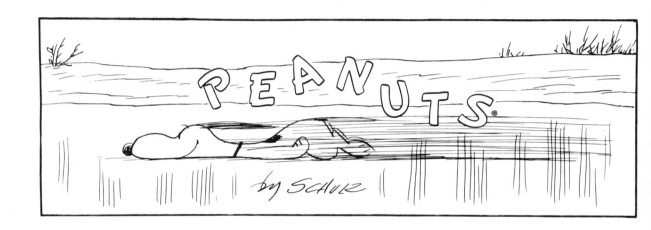

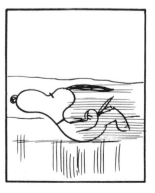

169

Maria's Idea

by DINA ANASTASIO

The Skateboard

Maria was riding her skateboard in front of the Mayor's offices when she heard about the medal. A woman and a man near her were talking.

"Why is the Mayor so mad all the time?" asked the woman.

"She thinks we all move too slowly," said the man. "Let's see, how did she put it? She said, 'It takes a week to get a day's work done around here.' She also said she'd give a medal to the one who could think of a way for us to move faster."

"That will be tough to do," said the woman. "Anyone who can help me move faster **should** get a medal." With that, she waved good-by and raced into the building.

A medal! Maria had always wanted to get something like that. Her big brother had won lots of things. His room was full of them. But Maria had never won a thing. She wanted that medal! All at once, she had an idea.

"You know what?" she said.

The man looked down at Maria and said, "What?"

"I know how the people who work here can move faster," said Maria.

"How?" he asked.

"Well," Maria said, "I think I'd better wait and tell the Mayor myself. I'd sure like to get a medal from her."

"I'll tell her for you," said the man. "Give me your name. I'll make sure the Mayor knows it's your idea."

Maria put her name and her phone number on a piece of paper. "Don't forget to give it to her," she said as she handed the paper to the man. Maria disliked him, but she told him her idea.

"Skateboards," Maria said. "The people in the Mayor's offices can ride on skateboards to move faster."

The man laughed. Then he said, "O.K., I'll be sure to tell her."

That night, Maria sat beside her phone. She waited and waited for the Mayor to call and thank her. But her phone didn't ring. Not once. Her phone did ring many times the next day. And the next . . . and the next. But Maria never got a call from the Mayor.

Then, one night when Maria was reading the paper, she found out why. The paper said:

MAYOR'S OFFICES TAKE UP SKATEBOARDING

Under it, there was a picture of the Mayor riding a skateboard. The paper went on to say that all the people who worked in the Mayor's offices were now moving fast. They were taking their reports to the Mayor on skateboards. The Mayor was very pleased.

As Maria read the story, her stomach started to turn. And by the time she had read all of it, she felt terrible all over.

This is what she read:

The skateboard idea came from Mr. Mack Mean, who works for the Mayor. Next week, Mayor Brown will give Mr. Mean a medal for the idea.

At the very end of the story, there was a small picture of Mack Mean. Maria looked at the picture. It was the man she had talked to in front of the Mayor's offices! She had told her idea to him!

"**Mean!**" Maria said out loud. "You can say **that** again." She had been right to dislike him. Then she put the paper away and thought. What could she do? She could call the Mayor and say that it had been her idea. But Maria knew that the Mayor would never believe her.

So Maria didn't do a thing but act very mad at supper that night.

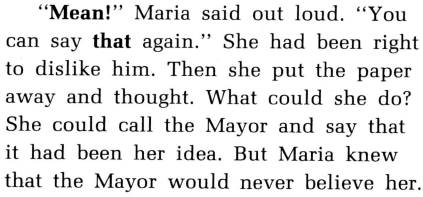

Best Idea of the Year

Maria thought about her skateboard idea all the next day.

When the paper came, she took it up to her room and read it. This time the paper said:

MAYOR'S OFFICES COME TO A STOP!

The story went on to say that all of the people in the Mayor's offices were too busy doing skateboard tricks. There was no time left to work. Maria read the rest of the story.

177

"Get rid of those skateboards!" the Mayor was heard to tell her workers. "They were a bad idea."

Then the Mayor called in Mr. Mack Mean, who had first thought of the skateboards. Mr. Mean stated, "The idea really wasn't mine. It was a little girl's." He gave the Mayor a piece of paper that, he said, had the girl's name and phone number on it. The Mayor has said that she will look into it.

As she was reading, Maria's stomach started to feel terrible again.

That night, when Maria didn't want her phone to ring, it did. It was the Mayor. "So it was your idea," she said.

"Well, kind of," Maria said.

"I'd like to talk to you," the Mayor said. "Can you come see me tomorrow?"

"Well, I think I can," Maria said.

"Good," the Mayor said. "I'll see you at one, Maria."

Maria didn't sleep much that night. Skateboards and medals and mayors were jumping in and out of her head.

The next morning, Maria thought of riding her skateboard to the Mayor's office. But she knew that wasn't a good idea. As she was late, she put on her rusty old roller skates.

When she got to the building, she was glad she had on her roller skates. The building was so big! Maria got to the Mayor's office just in time.

The Mayor was reading something when Maria skated in.

"Skateboards! What a silly idea!" the Mayor said, looking up. But she wasn't really mad.

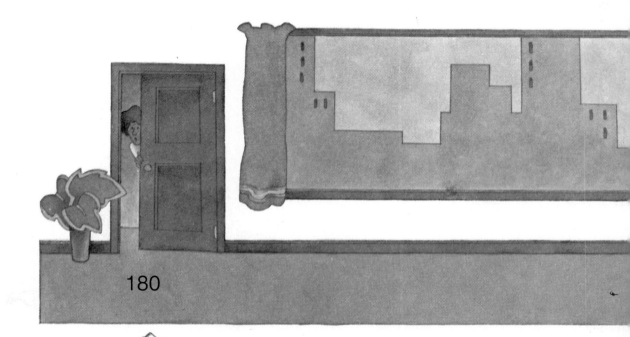

"I thought it was a good idea at first," Maria said. She skated over and sat down in a chair.

"Don't you ever walk, Maria?" the Mayor asked, looking at Maria's feet.

"Not if I can help it," said Maria. "It's too slow."

The Mayor looked at Maria.

Maria's stomach started to feel funny again.

At last, the Mayor said, "Can you do tricks on those things?"

"Not really," Maria said. "Not like you can with skateboards."

"Good!" the Mayor said. "But you **can** go fast on them, can't you?"

"They're a little rusty, but they are fast," said Maria.

"Let me try them," said the Mayor. Maria bent down and took off her skates. She gave them to the Mayor.

The Mayor put on the skates. She started to skate. At first, she skated slowly. Then she skated faster. Soon the Mayor was going as fast as Maria ever had.

"This is **it**, Maria!" the Mayor shouted as she flew by. "This is the answer to the problem!"

At last, she slowed to a stop. She took off the skates and handed them back to Maria. "Can you be here tomorrow at one?" she asked Maria. "I'd like to give you something."

"Yes," Maria said, smiling. She thought she knew what the Mayor would give her.

At one the next day, Maria skated
into the Mayor's office. The Mayor
smiled and gave her a bright gold
medal. She read the words on it.

TO MARIA FOR THE
BEST IDEA OF THE YEAR

Maria looked up at the Mayor and
said, "Oh, thank you! I've always
wanted a medal."

The Mayor smiled. Then she said, "Now, take off those roller skates."

"Why?" asked Maria. "I never walk if I can help it."

"This is why," the Mayor said. She handed Maria two golden roller skates.

Maria couldn't say a word. She put on the beautiful golden skates and smiled and smiled.

She skated home on her golden roller skates as if she were flying. Heads turned as she flew past.

When she got home, her brother said, "Golden roller skates **and** a medal! That's really something."

Now, all the people in the Mayor's offices take their reports to her on roller skates. And the Mayor smiles all the time. She says, "With roller skates, people do a week's work in a day!"

The Wheels of the Bus

The wheels of the bus go
round and round,
  Round and round, round and round,
  The wheels of the bus go
round and round,
  All on a busy morning.

The people on the bus go
up and down,
  Up and down, up and down,
  The people on the bus go
up and down,
  All on a busy morning.

186

The driver on the bus says,
"Move on back,
Move on back, move on back."
The driver on the bus says,
"Move on back,"
All on a busy morning.

The horn on the bus says,
"Toot, toot, toot;
Toot, toot, toot; toot, toot, toot."
The horn on the bus says,
"Toot, toot, toot,"
All on a busy morning.

Things That Are Alike

Things are often like other things. Read the sentences below. Can you tell what the missing word is? Can you tell why that is the right word?

<u>Socks</u> go with <u>feet</u> the way <u>mittens</u> go with _____.

    ears   hands   eyes

<u>Fish</u> swim in the <u>sea</u>, and <u>birds</u> fly in the _____.

    earth   sea   air

<u>Loud</u> goes with <u>quiet</u> the way that <u>hot</u> goes with _____.

    cold   big   old

In this story, Jill thought she saw how two things are the same.

Jill saw a picture of a knight. She said to Roberto, "Do you know what that picture of a knight makes me think of?"

"What?" asked Roberto.

"A turtle in its shell," said Jill.

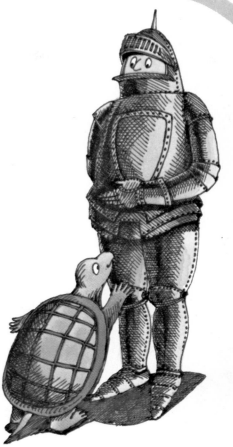

Why did Jill say that ? In what way is a knight like a turtle?

Sometimes you can work out a problem by thinking about things that are like the problem in some way. Read this story about Tom.

One morning, Tom got up and ran off to school. He did not stop to eat before he left.

189

Tom forgot to take his lunch with him. So he did not have anything to eat at noon.

By the time he left school, Tom was feeling terrible. He did not want to play ball. He did not want to sit and read a schoolbook.

"I must be getting sick," said Tom. "I feel like going home and going to bed."

Near his house, Tom saw Mr. Brown, his neighbor. Mr. Brown was standing next to his car, looking very sad.

"What is wrong?" said Tom.

"I forgot to get gas for my car," said Mr. Brown. "A car needs gas, or it will not go."

Tom looked at the car. And all at once Tom knew why he was feeling tired and sick. And he knew just what to do about it when he got home.

What did Tom think when he saw Mr. Brown's car?

What did Tom do when he got home?

Sometimes finding things that are alike in some way can give us good ideas. Look at the pictures. Can you see how they are the same?

Can you tell how each set of things is like the set next to it?

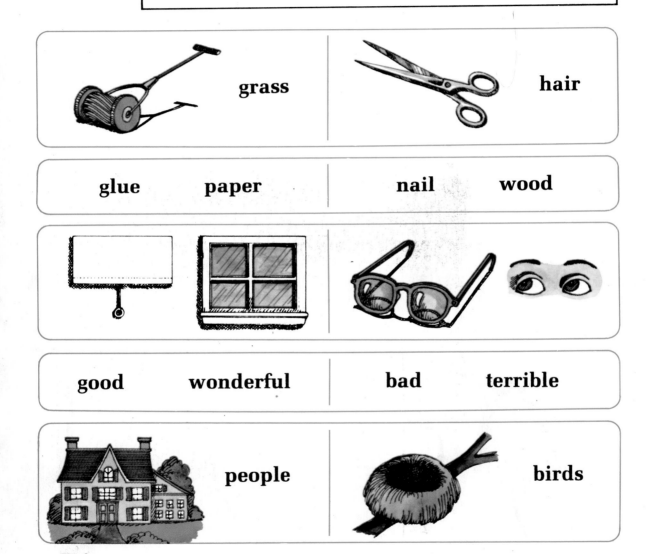

grass · hair

glue · paper · nail · wood

good · wonderful · bad · terrible

people · birds

Once Upon a Time

Tell Me a Story

Tell me a story
    Of castles and kings,
Of wizards and princesses,
    Magical things.

And when it is over
    And I am in bed,
The story keeps going
    Inside of my head.

ALICE LOW

The Giant Beet

Once upon a time, a poor woman planted some beet seeds. Only one of the seeds grew. But that beet grew so fast that the woman could see it get bigger. Soon it was as tall as a tree.

As the days went by, she watched the beet grow bigger and bigger. It got redder and redder. The beet was so big that the woman could not believe her eyes. It was indeed the biggest, finest beet the woman had ever seen.

195

"What can I do with a giant beet?" thought the woman. "I could never bring myself to sell a beet as grand as this. It's much too grand to be used as food. What terrible luck for a poor woman like me!"

Day and night the woman thought about her giant beet. At last, she had an idea.

"Why, I'll give it to the queen!" she said. "She should be pleased to have it. I'll put it in my wagon and take it to her castle."

The woman put the beet into her two-wheeled wagon. She climbed on top of her giant beet. Then the old wagon, pulled by her two old horses, went slowly up the path.

When the queen saw the beet, she stared at it, open-mouthed. Could it be real?

"This beet is much too grand for me," the woman said to the queen. "I will give it to you, for it is the finest beet in the world."

"Indeed it is," said the queen. "I am proud and happy to have it."

Then the queen stared at the good woman. How poor she looked! But here she was, giving away the finest thing she had.

The queen wished to thank the
woman for being so kind and good.
She wanted to be fair to her. So she
gave the woman a new house and
some rich land. She also gave her two
strong horses to help with the farming.

Now it happened that the poor woman had a rich brother. He was not only rich, but also very greedy. When he heard about his sister's good luck, he grew very angry.

"It isn't fair! Why should my sister have all the good luck?" he said. "Just because she gave the queen a big old beet? I can think of better things than beets to give the queen. I'll give her my finest horse."

Tickled by this idea, he lost no time. He got into a fine wagon. It was pulled by two old horses. Then, with the best horse following, he hurried along the path to the queen's castle.

The queen took the horse, for it was indeed as fine a one as she had ever seen. She looked at the brother.

"I can see you do not need money or land," said the queen. "But I do want to give you something. I have it! I'll give you something very fine."

The greedy brother was so happy he could not say a thing. He waited with his mouth open to see what she would give to him.

The queen went on, "Yes, I will give you a giant beet! There it is! You must see that no other beet is so fine. And thank you for the horse."

The queen walked away with her new horse. And now the rich, greedy brother was very angry indeed. But there was only one thing to do. He put the big beet into the wagon and headed for home.

"Alas," he thought. "It's so unfair! My sister has all the luck. This giant beet that made her rich has made me poor. Because of it, I have lost my very best horse."

The Elves and the Shoemakers

Act 1
The Surprise

This is a play that is told in two acts. The people who are needed for the play are:

Storyteller   A Man
Shoemaker Husband   A Woman
Shoemaker Wife   Two Elves

STORYTELLER: Long ago and far away there lived a husband and wife who made shoes. They were very poor.

HUSBAND: Oh my! No one buys our shoes any more. We have almost no money left.

WIFE: But we still work hard. Maybe we will have better luck soon.

HUSBAND: The harder we work, the poorer we get. Now we have only enough leather for one more pair of shoes.

WIFE: We still have a little money, dear. Come, let us go to sleep.

HUSBAND: You go to bed. I'll stay up and cut the leather.

STORYTELLER: The wife went out. The husband worked for a long time on the leather.

HUSBAND: All the leather is cut. I'll finish the shoes in the morning. I'll leave my tools on the bench.

STORYTELLER: The husband rubbed his eyes and went off to bed. The next morning, his wife came into the room. She spied a pair of shoes on the bench.

WIFE: Why, these shoes are the best he has ever made!

HUSBAND: Good morning, dear. I must get to work on the shoes.

WIFE: But the shoes are finished.

HUSBAND: You must be wrong. All I did last night was sit at the bench and cut the leather.

WIFE: But . . . but you **must** have made them! I know **I** didn't. Look!

HUSBAND (looks at the shoes): Can I make shoes in my sleep? Who could have made them? What a fine piece of work!

WIFE: Put them on the shelf in the window! Maybe someone will come in and buy them.

STORYTELLER: The shoemaker carried the shoes to the window. Soon a man rang the bell and came in.

MAN: I saw the beautiful shoes in the window. I must buy them for my wife.

HUSBAND (gets the shoes): Here they are, sir.

MAN: Never have I seen such fine
    shoes. I'll pay you three pieces of
    gold for them. Is that enough?
WIFE and HUSBAND: Oh, yes!

(The man pays for them and goes
out.)

WIFE: That's far more than we have
    ever gotten for one pair of shoes.
HUSBAND: Now we can buy enough
    leather for two more pairs. I'll cut
    them out tonight and work on them
    tomorrow.

STORYTELLER: Again, the husband cut the leather and left it on the bench. The next morning, they found **two** pairs of shoes had been made out of the leather.

HUSBAND: I can't believe my eyes! It happened again last night! Someone came in, used the tools, and made more shoes for us. Who could it have been?

WIFE: I don't know, but they are just as beautiful as the first pair. I'll put them in the window.

STORYTELLER: They sat down to wait. At once the door opened. A woman and two girls came in.

WOMAN: Oh, may we please look at those pretty shoes we saw in the window? They are just what my little girls like.

WIFE: Here they are.

WOMAN: I have never seen such fine
shoes! I'm sure my girls will love
them. I'll pay you ten pieces of gold
for them. I'll be sure to tell my
friends to come here to buy shoes.
WIFE: Oh, thank you very much!

(She waves as the woman leaves.)

HUSBAND: Our luck is getting better.
Now I can buy enough leather for
many pairs of shoes. Soon the
shelves will be filled with shoes.
We will be rich!

WIFE: Yes! Come, let us dance.

HUSBAND: Yes, let's dance.

(They dance together.)

HUSBAND (stops dancing): Still, I would
like to know who is making the
shoes each night.

WIFE: So would I. It is very odd. Do
you think we will ever know?

End of Act 1

Act 2
The Tiny Shoemakers

STORYTELLER: As time went on, the husband and wife wondered more and more about who was making the pairs of shoes. One cold night, in the dead of winter, the husband had an idea.

HUSBAND: I'm going to stay down in the store all night. I must find out who is making all those shoes.

WIFE: I'll stay with you. If we hide, we can keep our eyes on the bench.

HUSBAND: We must be still as mice!

WIFE: Yes!

STORYTELLER: That night, they waited in the dark. The store grew very quiet. Then, just at midnight, the lock on the door clicked. Two elves hopped in. They jumped on the bench and went to work.

ELVES: We tap, tap, tap
      On pieces of leather.
      We rap, rap, rap
      And put a shoe together.

HUSBAND (softly): Look at them!
    They're two tiny elves!

WIFE (softly): How happy they are!
    And how fast they work!

ELVES: We make a lot of shoes,
     And put them on the shelves.
     We dance a while,
     Two happy little elves!

STORYTELLER: The elves finished the shoes. They danced around as the husband and wife looked on. Then they ran to the door. The lock clicked as the elves went out into the night.

WIFE: Oh, the poor little elves. They went out into the cold winter night!

HUSBAND: Think how hard they have worked for us. How can we thank the little elves?

WIFE: Did you see how poorly they were dressed? Their clothes could never keep out the cold. I'll make little coats and caps for them.

HUSBAND: I'll make each one a pair of shoes. I'll use the very best leather I can buy.

STORYTELLER: The husband and wife set to work. They worked for days and days on the new clothes. At last they were finished.

HUSBAND: Look, dear! Tonight I will
put out these pairs of tiny shoes
in place of leather.

WIFE: And I'll put out the other clothes.

HUSBAND: Would you like to hide and
see the elves?

WIFE: Yes, dear, I would!

STORYTELLER: So once again the man
and his wife hid and waited. And
again, just at midnight, the two tiny
elves came. They went quickly to
the bench, looking for leather. How
happy they were to find, not
leather, but fine little clothes! They
quickly put them on, then danced
and sang.

ELVES: Now we are well-dressed
     little men.
    Never will we work again!

STORYTELLER: They sang the same little
    song over and over. Then they
    danced right out the door.

HUSBAND: I wonder, will those elves
    ever come back again?
WIFE: No, dear, I think not.

STORYTELLER: She was right. The elves
    never came back. But the husband
    and wife did not care. From that
    time on, they were happy and rich,
    thanks to the little elves.

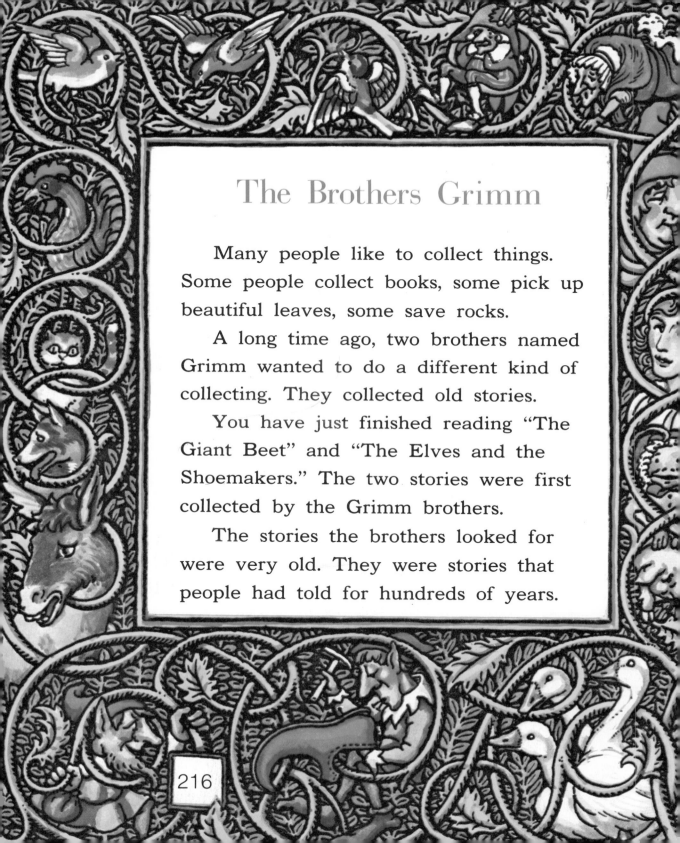

The Brothers Grimm

Many people like to collect things. Some people collect books, some pick up beautiful leaves, some save rocks.

A long time ago, two brothers named Grimm wanted to do a different kind of collecting. They collected old stories.

You have just finished reading "The Giant Beet" and "The Elves and the Shoemakers." The two stories were first collected by the Grimm brothers.

The stories the brothers looked for were very old. They were stories that people had told for hundreds of years.

No one knew when the stories were first told. Many of the people who told them could not read or write.

Fathers and mothers told the stories to their children. When the children grew up, they remembered the stories. They told the same stories to their children.

This went on for hundreds of years. But no one ever wrote the stories down.

As time went by, many people were taught to read. They started to read books filled with new stories. They stopped telling the old ones.

Soon only a few people remembered the old stories. And those people were growing older all the time.

The Grimm brothers were afraid that someday, when these people died, all knowledge of the old tales would die with them. That was why they wanted to collect the tales. But first they had to go find the few people who still remembered the stories.

And so with bags on their backs, the two brothers set out. They walked from village to village. They knocked on many doors. They worked hard to find persons who could remember and tell the old stories. Every time a tale was told, one of the brothers wrote it down.

Not all of the people were willing to tell their stories to two grown persons. One woman knew many tales. But she would tell her stories only to children. So the Grimm brothers brought a few young children to the woman's home.

As soon as the children were sitting around her, she said, "Once upon a time. . . ." Then she went on to tell story after story. One brother came in and hid. He wrote down the tales as she told them to the children.

After five long years of walking from village to village and from farm to farm, the brothers had collected almost one hundred tales. Their first book of old stories was soon printed. From the time that book came out, people everywhere enjoyed the tales.

The brothers collected other tales, until they had three books filled with more than two hundred stories. Today, children and grown-ups still enjoy the old tales. The stories collected by the Grimm brothers are printed and read just about everywhere in the world.

All Kinds of Reading

In the unit you have just read, all the parts were alike in one way. They were all about people and places of long ago. But they were different, too.

How is "Tell Me a Story" different from "The Giant Beet"?

How are they both different from "The Elves and the Shoemakers"?

Can you tell how "The Brothers Grimm" is different from all the others?

Even before you start to read, you can tell if you are going to read a poem, a play, or a story. You can tell just by looking at the page.

Look, and tell what each of these is.

When the grass starts to grow
And the warm winds blow
And the birds start to sing . . .
It's spring! It's spring!

PRINCE: I'm tired of being a prince. It's
   nothing but castles and gold and
   treasures all day long.
WIZARD: What would you like me to do
   about it?
PRINCE: How about turning me into a
   nice little frog?

Poems and plays are fun to read to yourself, but they are better if you read them out loud. Why do you think that this is true?

How are the two stories below different?

Once upon a time, in a land far away, lived a poor old farmer and his son. They worked very hard to grow enough food to eat.

When John Audubon was young, he loved to walk in the woods. He saw many kinds of birds and made about two hundred pictures of them when he was still a boy.

The first story is fiction. It is a story made up by a writer. The second story is fact. It tells true things.

What kind of book or story do you like to read? You can find almost any kind, if you look. There are books full of plays, or poems.

There are many books of fiction. And if you like to read facts about people and things, there are lots and lots of books you will like.

All you have to do is look!

Try This

1. Look quickly at the following pages in this book:

40   51   67   149   201

What is on each page, a poem or a play? How can you tell?

2. Read these pages to yourself:

111   130

Tell how the stories are different. Which story is fact? Which is fiction? How can you tell?

Collecting Things

Hopi: Heard Museum Phoenix
Pueblo Art USA 13c

Harriet Tubman

Black Heritage USA 13c

Stamps

Collecting Stamps

In the year 1840, the world's first stamps for letters were used in England. From that time on, many people all over the world have enjoyed collecting stamps. Boys and girls, and older people too, save them. They enjoy putting them in stamp books. Sometimes they trade them, too.

226

Why do so many people collect stamps? Some enjoy having sets of tiny colored pictures. Some like to collect things from faraway places. And some like to collect stamps because they are beautiful or rare.

It's easy to start collecting stamps. Ask your friends or your mother and father to save used envelopes for you. When you get some, keep the ones with stamps that you like.

Don't try to pull the stamps off the envelopes. Cut off the stamp corner of the envelope. Leave the stamp corner in water all night. By morning, the stamps will come right off the paper.

Then put the wet stamps on soft paper. Put more soft paper over them. Place a book on top to keep the stamps from curling as they dry.

227

When you have many stamps, you will want to sort them. They can be sorted by color, size, place, or by how much they sell for. They can also be sorted by the kinds of pictures on them.

You may want to keep your stamps in a stamp book. You can get one at a store. But if you don't want to buy a stamp book, you can make one from sheets of plain white paper.

Many people have enjoyed collecting stamps all their lives. You may, too.

Some of the World's Rare Stamps

This stamp was made to sell for two cents. It has a picture of a long train on it. The stamp was not made right. The picture is upside down. It was rare from the start because it was odd. And as time went by, its price soared. Today it sells for thousands of dollars.

This twenty-four-cent stamp has an upside down picture of a plane on it. Like the train stamp, this one was not made right. Today each of the stamps sells for tens of thousands of dollars.

This one-cent stamp was made in 1856. It is the only one left of its kind. Today it would sell for hundreds of thousands of dollars.

Maria Collects Seashells

Maria Lopez lives in a city far from the sea. But Maria collects seashells.

It all started last summer. Maria went to the beach with her mother and father for two days. She spent much of the time walking up and down the sandy beach, collecting shells.

The shells Maria picked up were once parts of living animals.

In the picture, you see a snail that lives in the water. The snail has hard and soft parts. The hard part is the shell, while the soft parts are inside the shell.

The shell is very helpful to the snail. When danger comes near, it just pulls in its head and hides inside the hard shell.

There are hundreds of different kinds of snails. Many of them have beautiful shells. Maria was very happy when she found the beautiful shells on the beach.

The shell of a sea snail is all in one piece. But a different kind of sea animal has a shell that is made up of two parts.

In the first picture, you see a clam with its two-part shell open. In time of danger, the clam can shut its shell and hide safely inside.

When sea animals like these die, only their shells are left. The waves of the sea carry some of the shells to the beach. The sun dries them. The wind and sand make them smooth and very shiny. There they stay on the sandy beach, until someone like Maria comes and collects them.

Maria keeps her shells in egg boxes. She puts the one-part shells in one box and the two-part shells in a different one. She would never think of mixing the two kinds of shells.

Maria sorts out the shells. Then she tries to find out everything she can about them. She studies books about seashells. She looks for pictures of the shells she found.

When she finds the name of one of the shells, she prints it on a piece of paper. Maria is hopeful that she'll soon have names for all the shells.

Then it will be time to return to the beach. It will be time to go back and look again for more of the beautiful seashells.

(To be read by the teacher.)

Shells

The bones of the sea
are on the shore,
shells
curled into the sand,
shells
caught in green weed hair.
All day I gather them
and there are always
more.

I take them home
magic bones of the sea,
and when
I touch one,
then I hear
I taste
I smell the sea
again.

LILIAN MOORE

Herbert's Treasure

by ALICE LOW

Herbert was a treasure collector.

He liked everything about collecting treasures.

He liked getting up in the morning and thinking about what he would find that day. He liked leaving his house and walking to the old junkyard. He liked looking in the big pile of junk near the old house. He liked finding treasures, bringing them home, and putting them in his room.

He liked looking at the treasures, too. Everywhere he looked in his room there was some kind of treasure. He had a hammer, a bird cage, some rope, and some wire, pieces of glass and a bicycle tire.

238

Herbert just liked having treasures.

His father and mother didn't like it at all. It was very hard to clean his room. Every week, day after day, they said, "Herbert, please, Herbert, throw something away!"

"I can't," said Herbert. "They're treasures."

"Junk!" said his mother. "Nothing but junk, Herbert!"

"You never know," Herbert said. "They just might come in handy — someday."

"This rusty can?" his father said.

"I can keep things in it," Herbert said. He picked up three shells, four nails, and a doorbell and put them in the can.

When his mother and father went out, Herbert took the treasures out of the can and looked at them. The doorbell didn't work, but it might — someday.

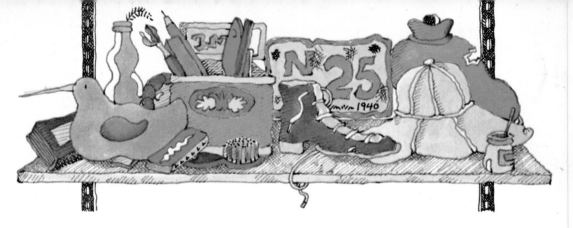

Every afternoon—in rain or sun—
when the other children were playing
ball, Herbert went to the old junkyard.
He went by himself, so he would have
all the treasures to himself.

One afternoon he found a rusty old
saw, some china and cans, a piece of a
pipe, and some paint pots and pans.
He carried them home.

His mother said, "Why do you go to
that place when our yard is so neat
and nice?"

"It's more fun in the junkyard,"
Herbert said.

"Get rid of that junk, Herbert, right
now, today," his father said. "Herbert,
throw something away."

"O.K.," Herbert said. "Tomorrow."

But the next day, Herbert brought
home a bent shovel, some chair backs,
and table legs. And a real find—a lock.
He put the new things on top of the
toys on the shelves.

"Now look at your toys!" said his
mother. "They're pushed under all that
junk. I mean it, Herbert, right now,
today. **Please,** Herbert, **please,** throw
something away."

"All right," Herbert said. He took
everything off the shelves and made
two piles—one to keep and one to
throw away. Then he got rid of the
throw-away pile.

After he'd put his treasures on the
toy shelves, he thought about the lock.
It didn't work, but it might—someday.

Every day Herbert brought home more — window panes, picture frames, wood from old floors, doorknobs, and boxes, and frames from old doors.

The mountain in the junkyard got smaller and smaller. And his room got fuller and fuller. Herbert had to make a path to get to his bed. And it was very hard to open the door.

It was fun to look around his room. But it was sad to go to the junkyard now because there was almost nothing left to find. The only treasure left was an old door.

Herbert pulled the door home on his wagon — slowly. He needed time to think about where he could put it. By the time he got to his room, he knew.

First he had to take out all of the treasures from under his bed. There was only one place to put **them** — on top of his bed. Then he put the door under his bed. That night he had to sleep on the chair.

The next morning, his father was very angry. He said, "This is it, Herbert! I mean it, today. Herbert, **please** Herbert, throw something away!"

"Don't worry, there's nothing more to find," said Herbert sadly. "But— maybe—there's something under the ground."

He set out with a shovel and started to dig. Digging was harder, but more fun, too. You never knew what might be under there.

Mostly there were rocks. Then one day the shovel hit something hard. It went **clang!** Metal! Only metal rang that way.

Herbert dug it up and shook off the soil. He washed it until he could see what it was. A key!

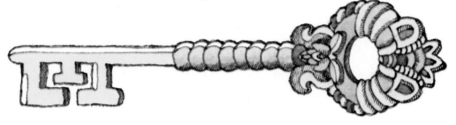

It didn't fit the back door, or the front door, or any other door. But it had to open something somewhere! Nobody would make a key that didn't open anything.

He put the key under his bed and thought about it every night. It might be the key to a box full of gold pieces. Then he could buy anything he wanted.

He'd like that. But where would he put all the new things?

Or maybe—this was still better—it was a key to a castle where he'd be the king. Not a castle full of gold, but a castle with nothing at all inside it, nothing but his treasures. And nobody else would live there.

It would be his own castle, where no one could say, "Herbert, **please,** Herbert, throw something away!"

Herbert could see it in his dream. He could see himself coming in the door with more and more treasures. The door was old and beautiful. No one else could open it because **he** had the key. He could see the lock, too. It was rusty and old.

Herbert opened his eyes. The moon was shining on the rusty lock. Herbert took out the key from under his bed. Slowly he tried the key in the lock. It didn't fit. Maybe the key was upside down. He turned it around. It still didn't fit. So he gave the lock a good shake and tried the key again. This time it fit! He turned it slowly. CLICK! The lock opened. The key fit the lock!

And the lock fit in the door! He hammered it in and put the doorknob on—and then he went back to sleep.

The next morning, Herbert got up and saw the door with the key in the lock. He remembered: it was going to be a busy day. He had a plan.

First, Herbert carried everything outside. His mother and father didn't ask what he was doing. They were just glad he was doing it—outside.

Herbert sawed and hammered for three days until he was almost done. Then he put on the door. And last, he opened the door with his key and moved everything in.

Then he hammered some more, and painted some, too. There were lots of shelves—shelves for his bird cage, his paint pots, and pans, his tire, and his wire, and his tools and his cans. And shelves for everything else.

Last of all, Herbert moved himself
in. It **was** a castle, just like the one in
his dream. The windows were cracked,
and the door made funny noises, but
there was lots of room—room for his
treasures, and no one to say, "Herbert,
please, Herbert, throw something away!"

The doorbell still doesn't work, but
it might—someday.

New Words

there
enough
almost
shovel
horn
dug
crash
seen
always

horrible
act
queen
tired
Bess
dear
princess
worry
carries
carrying
pear
dare

poor
hate

anything
somewhere
true
nobody
lonely
brought
else

Martha
Matilda
O'Toole
gate
she'd
taken
slate
won't
bit
I'd
hooted
forgot
roadside
pen
blackbird
flew
isn't
Sunday
rule

Simkin
Stanley
twenty
buying
few
Robinson
buffalo
greenhouse
Marcia
bonnet
ladder
another
Veronica
following
forty-seven
happily

kite
Pablo
high
watched
he'd
blew
branches
foot

above
taught
pool
you'd
shining
round

PAGES 98–103

Dipper
Alaska
state
everyone
fisherman
north
contest
flag
strong
fourth
July
parade

PAGES 104–110

maybe
our
Herbert
different
treasure
frames

doorknob
key
doorbell
letter
afraid

PAGES 111–117

dollar
darkened
porch
Norton
hurried
bill
crackled
pocket
snack
bar
money
table
bicycle

PAGES 118–125

storm
lawns
wind
Nell
Joshua
coat

crawled
fur
paws
closed
O.K.
held
purring

PAGES 130–137

balloon
ever
dream
Joseph
Montgolfier
parachute
also
smoke
answer
cloth
basket
brook

PAGES 138–147

village
trade
rest
rough
hurt

nothing
done
alas
popped
bought
whirled
stamped
threw

PAGES 150–154

whirlybirds
helicopter
metal
blades
straight
safely
traffic
police
freely
reports
helpful
place
cowboys
herd
unless
lucky
helpless
job

PAGES 155–167

cools
sailing
sailor
wheels
sand
flat
markers
touch
sled
ice
learning
gliders
pilot

PAGES 170–176

skateboard
mayor's
medal
week
tough
full
phone
number
disliked
stomach

PAGES 177–185

rusty
roller

PAGES 195–200

beet
path
stared
indeed
fair
greedy
angry
sister

PAGES 201–209

elves
shoemakers
husband
wife
leather
pair
finish
bench
spied
shelf
someone

rang
such
tonight
shelves

tiny
wondered
mice
midnight
lock
clicked
tap
rap
while
dressed
caps
sang
song

Grimm

collect
hundreds
write
wrote
someday
knowledge
every
everywhere
enjoy
printed

England
envelopes
corner
curling
sorted
upside
price
soared
thousands
cent

seashells
Lopez
sandy
snail
danger
smooth
shiny
everything
hopeful

collector
pile
wire
glass
handy
pans
panes
floors
mostly
clang
shake